RONAN O'CARROLL.

# ESSENTIAL PSYCHOLOGY

General Editor
Peter Herriot

## F3

## CLINICAL PSYCHOLOGY: THEORY AND THERAPY

# ESSENTIAL

# PSYCHOLOGY

# CLINICAL PSYCHOLOGY: THEORY AND THERAPY

**Dougal Mackay**

**Methuen**

First published in 1975 by Methuen & Co Ltd
11 New Fetter Lane, London EC4P 4EE
© 1975 Dougal Mackay
Printed in Great Britain by
Richard Clay (The Chaucer Press), Ltd
Bungay, Suffolk

ISBN (hardback) 0 416 82340 8
ISBN (paperback) 0 416 82350 5

We are grateful to Grant McIntyre of
Open Books Publishing Ltd
for assistance in the preparation of this series.

# Contents

# Editor's Introduction

Very many students of psychology choose clinical psychology as a career. Dougal Mackay's book succeeds admirably in providing an account of the current state of this rapidly changing applied area. He describes the historical development of the subject and how, in the past, clinical psychologists aimed to give a diagnostic assessment of patients with a view to establishing their pathological condition so that a psychiatrist could apply treatment. He goes on to assess clinical psychology's evolving role, in the context of various other conceptual frameworks than the medical model. Various current theories of personality are described, with the techniques of assessment and therapy associated with them. We get the feel of a process of radical change.

*Theory and Therapy in Clinical Psychology* belongs to Unit F of *Essential Psychology*. What unifies the books in this unit is the concept of change, not only in people but also in psychology. Both the theory and the practice of the subject are changing fast. The assumptions underlying the different theoretical frameworks are being revealed and questioned. New basic assumptions are being advocated, and consequently new frameworks constructed. One example is the theoretical framework of 'mental illness': the assumptions of normality and abnormality are being questioned, together with the notions of 'the cause', 'the cure', and 'the doctor-patient relationship'. As a result, different frameworks are developing, and different professional practices gradually being initiated. There are, though, various social and political structures which tend to inhibit the translation of changing theory into changing practice.

One interesting change is the current aversion to theoretical frameworks which liken human beings to something else. For example, among many psychologists the analogy of the human being as a computer which characterized Unit A is in less favour than the concepts of development (Unit C) and the person (Unit D).

*Essential Psychology* as a whole is designed to reflect this changing structure and function of psychology. The authors are both academics and professionals, and their aim has been to introduce the most important concepts in their areas to beginning students. They have tried to do so clearly, but have not attempted to conceal the fact that concepts that now appear central to their work may soon be peripheral. In other words, they have presented psychology as a developing set of views of man, not as a body of received truth. Readers are not intended to study the whole series in order to 'master the basics'. Rather, since different people may wish to use different theoretical frameworks for their own purpose, the series has been designed so that each title stands on its own. But it is possible that if the reader has not read psychology before, he will enjoy individual books more if he has read the introductions (A1, B1 etc.) to the units to which they belong. Readers of the units concerned with applications of psychology (E, F) may benefit from reading all the introductions.

A word about references in the text to the work of other writers – e.g. 'Smith (1974)'. These occur where the author feels he must acknowledge an important concept or some crucial evidence by name. The book or article referred to will be listed in the References (which doubles as a Name Index) at the back of the book. The reader is invited to consult these sources if he wishes to explore topics further.

We hope you enjoy psychology.

*Peter Herriot*

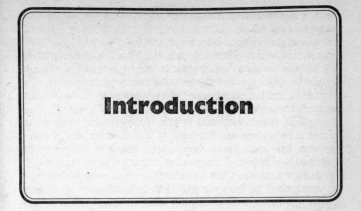

# Introduction

The purpose of this book is to introduce the student of psychology and the interested layman to the field of clinical psychology. This is not an easy task at this time because there is a lot of re-thinking and challenging of long-accepted views taking place, both inside and outside psychology and psychiatry. Inevitably, therefore, any account of current trends in this field must reflect the biases of the author. Since this book is no exception, I feel I should provide some information as to my general orientation at the outset.

In general, I find myself in sympathy with those theorists and therapists (see F1 and F8) who find the traditional medically oriented approach to be not only cumbersome, but also dangerously misleading in certain cases. It would seem to be far more appropriate to regard such problems as study difficulties, bereavement and marital discord as 'problems of living' (Szasz, 1960) rather than 'illnesses'. To me, the notion of illness implies a relatively discrete disease entity with associated signs and symptoms, which has a specific cause, a certain probability of recovery, and its own treatments. The various states of unhappiness, anxiety and confusion which we term 'mental illness' fall far short of these criteria in most cases.

Defenders of the medical position will, of course, argue that psychiatry is still a relatively young branch of medicine and that research will in time provide the answers. To those who are less committed to this conceptual framework, it would appear that the bulk of the research generated by the medical model has made only very limited advances to our state of knowledge in this field. They would argue that the disappointing results must indicate that the medical model is just not appropriate to handle this data.

It is, of course, one thing to argue that the medical model has no role to play in this context and quite another thing to argue the case for the model or models to replace it. The cognitive, interpersonal and behavioural schools have made great advances in the understanding and helping of those individuals whom psychiatric text books would describe as having a 'neurosis' or 'personality disorder'. Their progress however has been much slower with those who are termed 'psychotic'. Certainly the work of Laing has suggested that psychological approaches can benefit certain people who have been called 'schizophrenic' (see F8) and followers of Skinner have shown that long-term institutionalized cases can at least be trained to behave in a less bizarre fashion after a programme of operant conditioning (see A3). Nevertheless it must be conceded that, at this point in time, psychologists have little more understanding of the processes involved in these disturbances than the biochemists and physiologists who have been valiantly testing out their hypotheses for many decades. It may well be therefore that physical causes or at least involvements may be discovered eventually in some of those areas of disturbance which are proving resistant to psychological experimentation. Such findings, however, would not detract from the argument that the vast majority of people who go to their family doctor complaining of feelings of anxiety, unhappiness or confusion should not be regarded as 'ill'.

Despite the recent emergence of many schools who do not adhere to the concept of disease, there would appear to be some resistance on the part of society as a whole to the view that people who are locked up in institutions or sedated by their doctor may not in fact be ill but merely have a tendency to exhibit somewhat unusual, but perfectly valid, behaviour. Presumably the influential body of medicine, which has become so powerful in the last century or so, must take some responsibility for this in that it has done little to encourage these approaches which do not support the notion of illness.

Another factor, as experimental psychologists have repeatedly shown, is that people do not like to be faced with ambiguity. When we are faced with a situation we cannot make sense of, we tend to experience tension, and gravitate towards any labelling system which seems to provide meaning

10

for the incomprehensible. Thus the term 'mental illness' helps to reduce the discomfiture one experiences when faced with behaviour which deviates markedly from the norms. We can cope with those who behave in a markedly different fashion from us by dismissing them as 'sick'. If this label were to be removed or replaced by a more nebulous one, then all the unpleasant by-products of uncertainty would recur.

The further advantage of calling people 'sick' is that they can be placed in 'hospitals' for many years where they will be unable to upset their relatives, friends or members of the public with their bizarre behaviour. It is hardly surprising from this, therefore, that society wants to believe in the concept of 'mental illness' and does little to encourage more radical approaches to these problems.

At the same time, many of the people who have psychological problems derive a lot of comfort from the belief that they are 'sick'. This effectively means that they do not have to see themselves as being responsible for their own inadequacies. They can come along with their 'nerve trouble' to the hospital and expect to have everything put right by 'the doctor'. Thus when they fail to cope with a particular situation they can claim that it is due to this 'anxiety neurosis' which they have been told they have 'got', and really nothing to do with them as individuals. In this way they avoid responsibility for their actions. It is not surprising therefore to find that many people with problems are resistant to the suggestion that they are in no way 'ill'. Thus both society and the disturbed individual can be seen to be colluding with the medical profession to support the notion of 'mental illness'.

The history of psychiatry indicates that at any point in time there have always been labels available to refer to those whose behaviour is markedly eccentric. The type of label adopted has always depended on the particular *Zeitgeist* of the period. The medical advances of the last century have profoundly affected all our lives and so it is not altogether surprising that the label of illness is the one that is currently employed. However a brief résumé of the history of attitudes to those who behave strangely will, I hope, suggest to the reader that the present association between unusual behaviour and medicine is by no means an inevitable one.

The ancient Egyptians, Greeks and Hebrews generally took the view that any deviation from the normal could be attributed to the work of good or evil spirits. Not only were they thought to be responsible for eclipses of the sun, storms, earth-

11

quakes and other natural phenomena, but also for strange and unusual behaviour. If the signs of disturbance had a mystical flavour to them, then it was supposed that the individual had been visited by a 'good' spirit, and should therefore be treated with respect. If, on the other hand, the behaviour was deemed to be contrary to the teachings of the priests, then it was assumed that demoniacal possession had taken place. If the latter was thought to be the case, then extremely unpleasant measures were taken to expel these evil spirits from the body. Exorcism, which was the most commonly used ritual for this purpose, was practised exclusively by priests in their temples. As a rule this involved incessant chanting, starvation, flogging and other diverse tortures in order to drive the spirits out. As an alternative or in addition to exorcism 'trephining' was often attempted in order to expel these demons. This involved drilling a series of holes into the skull through which they could escape.

The notion that psychological disturbances were due to evil spirits was universally accepted until the dawn of the 'golden age' of Greece. Hippocrates, who is generally thought to be the father of medicine, is responsible for the beginnings of the association between psychological disturbances and medicine. He declared that these phenomena should be regarded as illnesses and that the cause of them lay in brain pathology rather than in demonology. Although his clinical descriptions of patients reveal that he had a clear understanding of the presenting problems, his views on aetiology indicate the degree of naivety of thinking in physiology at that time. He claimed that brain pathology was caused by disruption of the four body humours: blood, black bile, yellow bile, phlegm. Differences in presenting symptoms were thought to reflect the precise nature of the humoral disturbances. Treatment consisted of prescribing various drugs and purgatives which were thought to have their effect by altering the distribution of these fluids in the body. In addition, he recommended that the patients should be released from their dark cells and given facilities for exercise. This new medical approach spread to Rome where such noted physicians as Asclepiades and Galen put their recommendation into practice.

This early medical orientation towards disturbances of behaviour came to an end with the collapse of Greek and Roman civilization, and by the Middle Ages the notions of evil spirits and demons were very much in vogue again. In the early part of this period it was generally assumed that those who exhibited bizarre behaviour had problems of the soul, and consequently they were generally treated with kindness by members of the clergy. Exorcism at this time involved 'laying on of hands' and other gentle procedures. Later on in the Middle Ages there was a more widespread belief that they were in fact possessed by evil spirits and this led to a return to witchcraft and the occult. Once again it was believed that excessively cruel treatment of the individual was the only way to rid him of the evil spirits which were assumed to be possessing him. Thus such tortuous methods as flogging, immersion in hot water and confinement in chains were used once again to drive the demons out.

Such was the belief in official quarters that witchcraft was on the increase and responsible for the various storms and diseases which were prevalent at this time that a papal bull was issued in the latter part of the fifteenth century to encourage and assist the detection of witches. This was the first occasion when the Church officially stated its belief in the link between mental disorders and demonology. As an aid to witch-hunting, Pope Innocent VIII authorized the publication of a manual entitled 'Malleus Maleficarum' (the witches' hammer), which gave guidance as to how to conduct a procedure known as the Inquisition. This involved the hunting, diagnosing and persecution of witches. Those who were unfortunate enough to meet the criteria of witch were tortured unmercifully, mainly by burning, in an endeavour to extract confessions from them. This period was undoubtedly the lowest point in the history of psychiatry, at least from a humanitarian standpoint.

By the sixteenth century, with the emergence of the Renaissance, there was a general move away from the barbaric methods associated with witch-hunting towards the notion of mental illness. One of the early proponents of this approach was a Dutch physician called Johann Weyer who, while not altogether denouncing the importance of the supernatural in these matters, claimed that there was a whole variety of mental disorders which required treatment rather than exorcism. He was ahead of his time, however, and although he had several influential supporters James I ordered his books to be burned; they were also banned by the Church until this century.

At this time, institutions were gradually being set up throughout the world to cater exclusively for those with

13

mental disorders. In England, the monastery of St Mary of Bethlehem was converted to an asylum by Henry VIII in 1547. Its name in time became condensed to 'Bedlam' which is a term still in general use to refer to states of chaos or uproar. This institution was particularly renowned for its dreadful living conditions and the cruel practices employed by the staff. Members of the public used to pay in order to catch a glimpse of the more violent patients who were periodically on display. Similar conditions existed in other European institutions such as La Maison de Charenton in Paris and, more particularly, the Lunatic's Tower in Vienna.

It was not until the end of the eighteenth century that the Frenchman Pinel pioneered the humanitarian reforms which have persisted until the present day. He managed to persuade the French government to free some of the patients from La Bicêtre Hospital in Paris. To everyone's surprise, the liberated inmates did not go on the rampage but, on the contrary, remained very docile and frightened. This led to a change of attitude towards mental disorders and Pinel was subsequently permitted to implement his policies of kindness and consideration.

The treatment of mental disorders by showing kindness and consideration became known as 'moral therapy'. This involved treating the patients firmly at times, gently at other times, but always with dignity. Pinel's view of these people was that they were in fact essentially normal individuals who had lost the power to reason properly due to environmental stresses. By bringing them into institutions they would be leaving these factors behind them. This would lead to a reduction in their agitated state, after which they would be encouraged to discuss their problems both in individual and group settings. They were also encouraged to participate in various activities which are clearly forerunners of those currently carried out in occupational therapy. It is interesting to note here that many of the therapeutic communities which have arisen in recent years bear more than just a superficial resemblance to eighteenth-century moral therapy. It certainly proved to be very effective and the records demonstrate that the recovery rate was at least 70 per cent when this approach was at its peak.

Paradoxically it was the dramatic advances made in the medical sciences in the nineteenth century which led to the decline of moral therapy. The contributions of physiology, neurology and biochemistry to the understanding of physical

14

illnesses led to a strong belief that in time they would be able to make a similar contribution to 'mental illness'. Moral therapy was quickly dismissed as being too unscientific, medical superintendents were placed in charge of the institutions and attendants were replaced by nurses. Some support for the role of medicine in this field was provided by the findings that some mental disorders were in fact related to brain damage or brain diseases of various sorts. This was an encouraging start and it was therefore generally assumed at this time that the physical causes of the other disorders would soon be unearthed. With hindsight, it would now appear that a lot of this optimism was ill-founded. Despite enormous quantities of research, the bulk of 'mental illnesses' have defied any organic or biochemical explanation. Nevertheless the medical model is still very much with us and, despite the dearth of evidence to support the notion of illness, the majority of people with psychological problems are still receiving physical treatments such as drugs, electro-convulsive therapy and even brain surgery (see F8). It would be utter folly, however, to deny the existence of a lot of scientific evidence and imply that physical interventions are totally ineffective. There is no doubt that pharmacological agents, for instance, can change the individual so that his behaviour is less offensive to other people or so that he becomes less distressed by his problems. Whether this means that a 'cure' has been achieved, however, is very much open to question. Some existentialists would argue that, in certain cases, suicide could be seen as a valid piece of behaviour and that to regard suicidal tendencies as inevitably being symptoms of underlying psychopathology is to take a very narrow view of man. Certainly it would seem to many people that the widespread practice of prescribing tranquillizers to enable people to escape from their everyday worries is stretching the concepts of 'illness' and 'cure' to their limits.

Looking back at the history of psychiatry from ancient times to the present day, the striking feature is the way in which the generally accepted label for unusual behaviour has passed backwards and forwards between medicine and theology. Both schools of thought possess neat conceptual systems which allow members of society to dismiss those whose behaviour is unusual as 'sick' or 'possessed'. Fitting a person into such a category effectively reduces the need to understand and interact with him. However, neither model has been particularly successful so far as treatment is concerned.

15

Indeed it is interesting to note that 'moral therapy', as far as can be judged from historical documents, emerges very creditably in comparison with the other two in terms of both humanitarianism and efficacy.

Pinel's approach can be seen to be a precursor of some of the psychological approaches which are currently growing in popularity. His notion that those with psychological problems are 'normal' people who have reacted badly to stress is being expressed currently by psychological thinkers of diverse persuasions. Furthmore, the emphasis which many psychotherapists now place on getting their clients to participate more generally and be involved in solving their problems is in keeping with the general approach adopted in the Parisian hospitals of the eighteenth century. Nowadays, of course, psychological thinking is considerably more advanced and many of the psychosocial therapies which are currently in vogue have a lot to offer in addition to kindness and consideration. Thus, in view of the encouraging results apparently achieved by the naive psychological approach of Pinel, and in view of the current state of inertia induced by the medical model, a strong case could be argued for creating centres in the community run according to psychological principles. Whether society would relish the idea of having to cope with those who behave differently, without the defence of a labelling system, is another matter altogether.

In this book, as has already been indicated, the emphasis will be very much on the psychosocial models and associated therapies which are currently in vogue. There will be no attempt to cover in depth the full range of theories and therapies which can be subsumed under the general banner of psychiatry. For a more medically oriented review of the field of psychiatric disorders the reader is referred to Slater and Roth (1969).

# Part One
# The medical approach to psychological problems

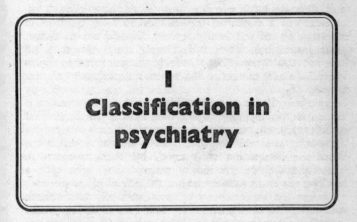

# I
# Classification in psychiatry

Systems of classification are useful in the sciences in that they provide a means whereby highly complex material can be rendered more manageable and subjected to experimental inquiry. The fact that an individual structure can be assimilated into a particular category on the basis of one or two variables enables one to make a prediction that it will possess some of the other attributes which are considered to be characteristic of this particular membership class. Thus psychologists and psychiatrists who favour a rigorous scientific approach have naturally expended a great deal of energy on developing taxonomic systems for dealing with the wide range of behavioural disturbances which are presented to them.

A classification system, of course, is only of any real value here if it provides the clinician with some knowledge as to possible causes, course of action and appropriate management of a particular type of disorder. It is therefore not surprising that neither the theologians nor the moral therapists took much interest in developing such a conceptual system. As far as the medieval priests were concerned, all psychological disturbances were seen as having a common cause (possession by the devil) and a common treatment (exorcism). This was administered to everyone who was seen to be afflicted in this way. Thus a list of the various types of disturbance would have contributed little to the understanding or management of the individual case. Pinel and his followers concentrated on creating a stress-free environment where each person could come to terms with his own particular problems, and it is doubtful whether they would have allowed the existence of a system of classification to have much of an influence on the way in which the individual was handled in their institutions. Thus it has really been the medically oriented practitioners who have been concerned to isolate various discrete categories of behaviour, analogous to physical illness.

The psychiatrist who undoubtedly laid the foundations of the currently employed classification system was Emil Kraepelin (1913). He pointed out that certain groups of signs and symptoms occurred together with sufficient regularity to merit the designation of 'disease'. He then proceeded to describe the diagnostic indications associated with each of the syndromes. In addition he saw the origins of the disorders as being due to hereditary diseases, metabolic disturbances and endocrine abnormalities. He found no place for psychological or sociological factors in the causality of these diseases. Furthermore he took a very deterministic position and stated that patients either naturally recover or inevitably deteriorate, depending on the nature of their disease. Although his over-emphasis on organic factors and fatalism regarding outcome are not shared by even the most organic of contemporary psychiatrists, his comprehensive classification system, with some major modifications, is still adhered to by clinicians throughout the world.

There are generally considered to be five major types of psychiatric disorders. These are:

  (i) the neuroses
 (ii) personality disorders
(iii) functional psychoses
(iv) organic psychoses
 (v) mental retardation

In the following pages, some of the most common examples of each category are defined and described.

Before dealing with these various disorders, it is necessary to make a brief comment regarding the style in which they are presented. Although it is not in keeping with the general theme of this book to talk about people experiencing 'symptoms' and demonstrating 'signs' of 'mental illness', it would be extremely tedious for the reader were these medical expressions to be translated or qualified repeatedly throughout the remainder of this chapter. In the interests of simplicity, therefore, the medical format and language will be adopted.

## The neuroses

The individual is considered to be neurotic if he experiences anxiety in situations which do not generally evoke such a reaction. He attempts to cope by avoiding, both in his thoughts and his behaviour, the causes of his distress. Although much of his behaviour may seem to be maladaptive, he does not exhibit the bizarre and violent behaviour which is characteristic of other psychiatric disorders. Instead he appears as an unhappy and guilt-ridden person who is ineffective in both work and social situations.

The *neurotic paradox* is an expression used to refer to the self-defeating strategies adopted by patients in this category. At first sight it appears puzzling that an individual should cling to thinking and behavioural patterns which ultimately bring distress and unhappiness. The explanation most favoured by psychologists is that these coping mechanisms bring him relief from anxiety in the short term. In addition, it follows that since he is always avoiding, he never allows himself to test out the situation to determine how stressful it actually is. In other words, the seemingly paradoxical behaviour of the neurotic, in making himself more and more upset by irrational or exaggerated fears, can best be understood in terms of his desire for immediate tension release.

### Anxiety neurosis
*Definition.* One of the most lucid descriptions of anxiety neurosis or 'free-floating anxiety' as it is sometimes called is that provided by the American Psychiatric Association (1968):

This neurosis is characterized by anxious over concern extending to panic and frequently associated with somatic symptoms. Unlike 'phobic neurosis', anxiety may occur under any circumstances and is not restricted to specific situations or objects. This disorder must be distinguished from normal apprehension or fear, which occurs in realistically dangerous situations. (p. 39)

*Clinical picture.* The patient with anxiety neurosis typically has some or all of the following symptoms:

1 inability to concentrate
2 difficulty in making decisions
3 sleep disturbances
4 overactivity of the autonomic nervous system (see A2), e.g. rapid heart beat, palpitations, excessive sweating, nausea, gastrointestinal distress, severe headaches, excessive muscle tension.

Patients who fit into this category are directly experiencing all the discomfiture generated by their anxiety, unlike other neurotics who have developed some strategy which prevents them from feeling the psychological and physical pain. Those who suffer from 'free-floating anxiety' tend to experience persistent tension which is interrupted from time to time by acute panic attacks. The misuse of alcohol or other drugs by these patients in order to alleviate the immediate stress can sometimes complicate the clinical picture.

*Phobias*
*Definition.* A phobia is a persistent fear of a specific object or situation for which there is no rational basis. The patient himself typically recognizes that there is no danger but this awareness in itself does nothing, as a rule, to alleviate his distress. Phobias may involve stimuli which do not normally evoke a fear reaction (e.g. birds), or they may concern situations which make most people a little uneasy (e.g. flying). These are a few of the more common phobic stimuli with their diagnostic labels:

acrophobia – heights
agoraphobia – open space
claustrophobia – closed space
monophobia – being alone
pathophobia – disease
pyrophobia – fire

*Clinical Picture.* The patient usually has many of the autonomic disturbances which are characteristic of anxiety neuroses, but in this case the symptoms are only experienced when he is faced with certain specific objects or situations. These physical symptoms of anxiety range from mild discomfort to vomiting and fainting.

There has been much discussion in the literature recently as to whether the disorder of agoraphobia should really be considered a bona fide phobia. This problem has arisen largely because clinicians have tended to make use of this diagnosis with people who are terrified to leave their house. A close examination of their complaint would undoubtedly reveal that, in the majority of cases, it is not the 'open space' factor which is causing the anxiety but the thought of facing the outside world. Thus the term phobia hardly seems appropriate unless it can be accepted that 'the world outside my house, constitutes a specific situation. Increasingly, psychiatrists have come to accept the views of clinicians such as Snaith (1968) who suggests that this misleading diagnostic label should be replaced by 'non-specific insecurity fears'. Thus it would appear that the various problems encompassed by the term agoraphobia are more akin to anxiety neurosis than to phobic states, in the majority of cases. The term should be reserved for that relatively small group of people who really do experience anxiety in wide open spaces.

*Obsessive-compulsive neurosis*
*Definition.* The patient with obsessive-compulsive neurosis experiences persistent thought patterns which he tries to prevent (obsessions) and repetitive tendencies to behave in a way which he does not wish to (compulsions).

*Clinical picture.* Some of the more common obsessions include such diverse topics as exaggerated concern regarding bodily functions, repeated attempts to solve problems, or strong tendencies to commit immoral acts of various sorts. Probably the most frequently occurring compulsions are those concerned with washing or toilet rituals. Typically the patient feels that he has to count up to certain numbers when washing his hands and his face in order to be free from contamination. If he is interrupted then he experiences an overpowering urge to go back to the beginning and start all over again.

The essential feature of obsessive-compulsive disorders is that the ideas or impulses to action occur with 'a subjective

21

sense of compulsion overriding an internal resistance' (Slater and Roth, 1969). This resistance is seen to be the important distinguishing feature between an obsessional thought pattern and a delusional system. Thus if the patient is totally overwhelmed with ideas of contamination, and does not feel them to be irrational, then the diagnosis of obsessive neurosis would not be applied and that of schizophrenia given serious consideration.

## Neurotic (reactive) depression

*Definition.* In the case of reactive depression the individual's symptoms of extreme dejection are seen to be a response to some stressful event or series of upsets.

Traditionally, psychiatrists have attempted to make a distinction between neurotic and psychotic (endogenous) depression. There are now many who would argue that the dividing line is far from clear (Kendall, 1968) and that depression should be regarded as a unitary disorder. For present purposes, the two types of depression will be presented with their presumed-to-be distinct clinical features.

*Clinical picture.* The major symptoms which would enable one to make a diagnosis of 'neurotic depression' are as follows:

1 subjective report of unhappiness
2 inability to face the future
3 lack of energy
4 difficulties in concentration
5 pre-occupation with unpleasant thoughts
6 difficulties in getting off to sleep

It should not be assumed that all depressives walk around in a slumped and dejected fashion, with facial expressions telegraphing their feelings of deep despondency. Many depressives manage to take an active part in conversations, smile when appropriate and even recite jokes in order to present a good front to their friends, colleagues, spouse and sometimes even to their family doctor.

## Hysterical neurosis (conversion type)

*Definition.* Traditionally the diagnosis of conversion hysteria is used with those conditions where the symptoms of some physical illness appear in the absence of any organic pathology. According to Freud, the signs of disturbance are merely manifestations of unresolved sexual conflicts. In his

22

view, the anxiety elicited by such matters is *converted* into a physical form. Although few contemporary clinicians would support such an explanation, the term conversion hysteria is still widely used. As well as providing the individual with release from psychological tension, it is claimed that the symptom benefits the individual in other ways. This 'secondary gain', as it is called, refers to the fact that the individual may acquire the attention he craves for, or may avoid an unpleasant situation, by consciously developing his particular symptom. Since it is often difficult to determine any 'gain' the individual may be deriving from his symptoms, most psychiatrists regard this aspect as a common but not essential feature of hysteria.

*Clinical picture.* The physical symptoms of conversion hysterics can usefully be considered under three main headings: sensory, motor and visceral.

1 *Sensory symptoms:* Two of the more common types of reactions involving these senses are *anaesthesia* (complete loss of sensitivity to pain) and *paresthesia* (tingling or other unusual sensations). More dramatic disorders of this type which have been reported are *hysterical blindness* (Parry-Jones *et al.*, 1970) and *hysterical deafness* (Malmo, 1970).
2 *Motor symptoms:* The psychoanalytic literature contains many reports of cases of hysterical paralysis, where the patient has lost the use of an arm or leg because of psychological disturbances (e.g. Abse, 1959). Disturbances of speech such as *aphonia* (inability to talk above a whisper) and *mutism* (complete inability to talk) are other examples of motor types of hysterical disorders.
3 *Visceral symptoms:* Pseudo-cases of appendicitis, malaria, tuberculosis, and pregnancy demonstrate the extent to which conversion disorders can simulate organic conditions. Far more common are the coughing fits, black-outs and severe headaches to distinguish many of these disorders from psychosomatic illnesses such as asthma or migraine which many would argue are partially caused by psychological factors.

There are three features of hysterical conversion disorders which have been variously proposed to assist the clinician in distinguishing them from organic and psychosomatic illnesses. These are:

1 'la belle indifférence' – lack of concern about symptoms
2 selective nature of the dysfunction – e.g. inability to speak in the presence of certain people
3 inconsistency in symptomatology – e.g. paralysed arm which does not atrophy.

Useful as these guidelines are, the differential diagnosis issue, particularly with those patients who have more than a superficial knowledge of medicine, can prove to be problematic.

## Hysterical neurosis (dissociative type)
*Definition.* The disorders referred to as hysterical dissociative type occur less frequently but are even more theatrical than the conversion type. As the name might suggest, it is used in those cases where the patient attempts to escape from stress by cutting himself off in some way or other. As a result, he is able to deny responsibility for his behaviour.

*Clinical picture.* There are thought to be four basic types of hysterical dissociative disorder: somnambulism, amnesia, fuge and multiple personality.

1 *Somnambulism:* The sleepwalker typically gets out of bed in order to perform certain acts in connection with his dreams. He returns to bed and continues to sleep as if nothing has happened, as a rule. He has no recollection of his nightly activities when questioned.
2 *Amnesia:* Hysterical amnesia, as opposed to that which has an organic basis, refers to the inability to recall certain events from the past. It differs from the organic type in that the hysteric is very often able to recognize the material when it is presented to him whereas the brain-damaged patient is unable to recollect anything about an event, despite a great deal of prompting.
3 *Fugue:* A fugue is an extension of the amnesic state and involves a 'flight' from one's problems. Typically the patient wanders off on a journey and, perhaps after several weeks, finds himself in a strange place with no recollection as to how he arrived there.
4 *Multiple personality:* Frequently referred to erroneously by the layman as schizophrenia (i.e. split personality), this very rare and fascinating disorder involves the patient having two or more quite distinct personalities. At any one

time, the individual has no knowledge of the existence of the other personality.

The common feature of these four disorders is that patients who have them think and act perfectly normally. If it were not for the fact that they are unable to recall certain very important events or facts regarding themselves, they would in no way be regarded as being mentally ill.

Other types of neurosis which have been omitted because of space include *neurasthenia* (chronic lack of energy), *depersonalization* (persistent dream-like state), *anorexia nervosa* (absence of any desire to eat) and *hypochondriasis* (oversensitivity regarding bodily functions). For a description of these disorders and some additional ones as well, the reader is referred to Slater and Roth (1969) and Coleman (1972).

## Personality disorders

Whereas there is the common thread of anxiety running through the various disorders described as neurotic, there is no such clear-cut feature in the case of the so-called personality disorders. In view of the somewhat nebulous descriptions of this heterogeneous group of disorders, many psychiatrists find themselves unable to fit the patient into a particular grouping, and even when they can do so with some confidence, feel that little is gained by this naming exercise in terms of understanding the nature of the problem. To say that someone is not coping because of an 'inadequate personality' is clearly verging on the tautological.

The only disorder in this major category which is presumed to have some of the characteristics of a syndrome is the 'psychopathic personality'. A description of this disorder is followed by a brief comment about some of the other, less clearly defined, abnormalities of the personality.

### Psychopathic personality
*Definition.* The Mental Health Act (1959) defines psychopathy as 'a persistent disorder or disability of the mind (whether or not including subnormality of intelligence) which results in abnormally aggressive or seriously irresponsible conduct on the part of the patient, and requires or is susceptible to medical treatment'.

There are one or two problems associated with this definition which require some elaboration. In the first place, by equating psychopathy with anti-social conduct, it effectively excludes the inadequate psychopath, who tends not to engage in overtly aggressive behaviour. In addition it fails to provide a clear-cut distinction between the psychopath and the psychotic, both of whom are capable of violent and anti-social behaviour. Finally the clause referring to the need for, or response to, treatment is not particularly helpful to the clinician who is attempting to formulate a diagnosis. Thus to say that to classify someone as having an illness he has to require treatment is, in effect, to say very little. Similarly, the fact that the label should be used to classify people who are 'susceptible' to treatment, means that the diagnosis can only be applied confidently in retrospect. But surely one of the main purposes of diagnosis is to enable the clinician to predict the response to treatment of the individual patient. Unfortunately, inadequate medico-legal definitions of this kind are by no means the exception to the rule in this field.

*Clinical features.* Psychopaths are usually found to be of above average intelligence and very likeable on first acquaintance. This attraction, however, tends to pall after a while as their utter disregard for the rights and needs of others becomes more apparent. Psychopaths appear in many shapes and forms and the diagnosis is certainly not confined to those who engage in criminal activities. The worlds of entertainment, politics and big business, for instance, are considered to have more than their fair share of psychopaths. The following features are considered to be characteristic of psychopathic personalities:

1 absence of guilt – lack of moral and ethical values
2 impulsivity – failure to look beyond the present
3 stimulus-seeking – need for excitement
4 low frustration tolerance – cannot delay gratification
5 inability to profit from experience – punishment does not change behaviour
6 socially skilled – his charm tends to disarm even those who have been misused by him
7 inability to maintain relationships – cannot give or receive affection of any depth

Some authorities claim that there are three different types of psychopath. The *aggressive* psychopath carries out violent deeds or is, at least, persistently verbally abusive. The *in-*

*adequate* psychopath is rarely aggressive and is depicted as lacking in foresight, possessing anti-social feelings and having the becoming manner which is so much a feature of this disorder. The *creative* psychopath, a type which is by no means universally accepted, uses his guilt-free insensitive qualities in a way that society would judge to be creative. Examples of creative psychopaths include the 'B' movie 'mad scientist' who produces monsters or secret weapons without regard for their consequences, and the leader in time of war who is regarded as 'sick' in times of peace.

## Miscellaneous personality disorders

As stated above, the traditional classification of many so-called personality disorders is regarded by many psychiatrists as having little value. For this reason these disorders will be dealt with very briefly. Many of them have features in common with other psychiatric disorders and it is often difficult to distinguish them from the 'illness' of the same (or similar) name. The most important are the obsessional, paranoid, schizoid and inadequate personality types.

The *obsessional* personality is characterized by rigidity of thinking, excessive conscientiousness and close adherence to rules and regulations. The *paranoid* personality is suspicious of other people and hypersensitive to criticism. This is usually accompanied by exaggerated feelings of self-importance and a tendency to blame others for one's own shortcomings (i.e. projection). Unlike the schizophrenic with the same name, the paranoid personality's behaviour can be understood if some knowledge of his background and present life situation is provided. The *schizoid* personality, although still in contact with reality, prefers to live in his own world of day-dreams and fantasies and avoids close interpersonal relationships. Finally, the *inadequate* personality is unable to cope intellectually, emotionally or physically with the demands being made on him from his environment.

## Functional psychoses

The psychotic is depicted as being considerably more disturbed than those described in the previous two groups. The 'normal' layman can, to a certain extent, empathize with the person who is suffering under stress or who suffers no guilt while breaking the rules of society, but is generally unable to understand the person who has a totally different conception of reality. He is frightened by the behaviour of the psychotic and attempts to reduce this anxiety by calling him 'mad' or 'insane'. Labelling serves the purpose of rendering any further explanation redundant.

The following clinical signs are generally used in order to separate both the functional and organic psychoses from the neurotic and personality disorder groups:

1 denial that there is a problem
2 poor contact with reality
3 disorientation of place and time
4 likelihood of harming self or others

The functional psychoses are distinguished from the organic psychoses on the basis of presumed differences in aetiology. Whereas the physical causes contributing to organic psychoses are beyond dispute, there is no tangible evidence, as yet, that there are biological determinants of the functional psychoses despite the innumerable and diverse hypotheses which have been put to the test. It is because it is not unlikely that they may be caused largely by psychogenic factors that they have been kept separate and subjected to more psychosocially oriented experimentation. As yet, however, this line of research has proved no more productive than the medically oriented kind in unearthing causative factors.

It would be wrong, however, to assume that the prognosis is necessarily better for the functional disorders than for the organic ones. Thus, for instance, in those cases of schizophrenia where the onset is gradual and is seemingly unrelated to external factors, and where emotional flattening has been observed from an early age, the probability of recovery is very low indeed. On the other hand, many patients who demonstrate psychotic behaviour following injury to the brain recover sufficiently to lead a normal life, despite the fact that cerebral damage is irreversible. Therefore the major type of diagnosis which is allocated to a patient provides little indication as to the anticipated duration of the disorder.

The two main functional psychoses are *schizophrenia* and *manic-depression*:

### Schizophrenia
*Definition.* The term 'dementia praecox' (senility of youth) was adopted by Kraepelin to refer to a group of disorders which he saw as being characterized by deterioration in

cognitive, perceptual and emotional functioning, and which had their onset in childhood. Not long afterwards, the Swiss psychiatrist Bleuler pointed out that this designation was inaccurate for two main reasons. In the first place, he had observed that in many cases the disorder did not become apparent until adulthood and it would therefore be inappropriate, he thought, to see it as being exclusively a young person's illness. In the second place, he did not agree with Kraepelin's opinion that this disorder involved deterioration analogous to senile dementia. A process of slow, irreversible decline in psychological functioning did not accord with his observations of patients. He proposed, therefore, that the term 'schizophrenia' should be adopted instead, because of the 'splitting of the personality' aspect, which seemed to him to be such a central feature of the disease. Posterity has favoured Bleuler's position on this matter and Kraepelin's original term has become extinct.

The notion of split-personality requires some elaboration here because there has been a tendency for lay people to equate schizophrenia with the Dr Jekyll/Mr Hyde syndrome. This celebrated character from fiction is in fact an excellent example of the disorder of multiple personality (see p. 24) which is a neurotic as opposed to a psychotic disorder. In the case of multiple personality, two rational, coherent individuals are seen to exist within the same person, and the splitting refers to the division which exists between the two. In schizophrenia, the splitting involves a barrier between the individual and the outside world. The psychotic lives in his own version of reality and, as a result of this, behaves in a way which appears bizarre according to external standards. The notion of splitting in schizophrenia is also used to refer to a lack of congruence between the individual's thoughts and feelings.

To summarize, schizophrenia can be defined as a psychotic disorder, with no known organic basis, which involves personality disintegration and disruption of perceptual, cognitive and emotional functioning.

*Clinical picture.* Although not all schizophrenics show the same clinical features, the following disturbances are considered by such authorities as Slater and Roth (1969) to be the 'essential psychological abnormalities':

1 *Thought process disorder.* By this is meant the inability to

keep to the point, the tendency to follow side issues, and susceptibility to distraction from clang associations (e.g. thing, string, fling), alliterations and symbolic meanings associated with each word uttered.

2 *Disturbances of affect*. The two types of affective disturbances which are characteristic of schizophrenia are 'flattening of affect', where the patient apparently loses the capacity to experience certain emotions, and 'incongruity of affect', where the demonstration of emotion does not seem to be in keeping with his thoughts.

3 *Psychomotor disorders*. The occurrence of stupor, catalepsy (i.e. condition in which muscles are semi-rigid) or behavioural stereotypes (e.g. persistent pacing up and down), in the absence of brain damage or disease, is considered to be a strong indication for using a diagnosis of schizophrenia.

4 *Lack of volition*. Schizophrenics typically demonstrate an inability to make decisions or carry out a particular activity, usually because they do not feel that they are under their control.

5 *Primary delusions*. A delusion, which can be defined as a false belief that is maintained in the presence of contradictory evidence, is considered to be 'primary' where it does not constitute an attempt, on the part of the patient, to make sense of hallucinations he is experiencing.

6 *Hallucinations*. The perception of objects which are not present is the least important of the six criteria since it is a phenomenon not exclusive to schizophrenia. However there is a tendency for schizophrenic hallucinations to be of an auditory nature and organic ones to be visual.

There are generally considered to be four types of schizophrenia, which have been termed simple, hebephrenic, catatonic and paranoid. In each type one or more of the six primary symptoms is particularly predominant.

*Simple* schizophrenia is the most difficult of the four to diagnose since the more florid signs, such as delusions and hallucinations, are not found here as a rule. The most striking features are flatness of affect and lack of volition. In *hebephrenic* schizophrenia, disorders of thinking and emotional disturbances in the form of inappropriate silly giggles are the most pronounced symptoms. Psychomotor disturbances, such as remaining in a fixed position for several hours, is the major diagnostic indication for *catatonic* schizophrenia. This period of withdrawal is often followed by one of intense excitement, during which the patient may attack everything and everyone. The most homogeneous type of schizophrenia is the *paranoid* variety, where primary delusions, usually of grandeur and/or persecution, and hallucinations predominate.

The fact that paranoid schizophrenia is a relatively easily recognized disorder, whereas the other three have less distinct boundaries, has lead a number of research workers (e.g. Venables, 1963) to regard the paranoid/non-paranoid distinction as the only viable division in this field.

### Affective psychosis
*Definition*. By the term affective psychosis is meant a disorder where the disturbances of affect, which can range from extreme excitability to intense sadness, is the primary symptom from which all others are derived.

*Clinical picture*. The three types of affective psychosis which are generally recognized are mania, depression and the circular type of manic-depression.

The symptoms of *mania* are as follows:

1 denial of problems
2 elated mood (from infectious humour to wild excitement)
3 pressure of thoughts – constant high output of talk
4 flight of ideas – easily distracted by opportunities for punning and playing with words
5 short but intensive attention span
6 grandiose ideas – excessive self-conceit as opposed to delusions of grandeur
7 markedly decreased need for sleep
8 increased sex drive

A distinction is often made between *hypomania* (relatively mild elation) and *hypermania* (extreme excitement).

The symptoms of *endogenous depression*, which is arguable distinct from reactive depression (see p. 22) are quite the reverse of those associated with manic psychosis:

1 complaints of sudden loss of interest or drop in efficiency
2 low spirits unaffected by change in environment
3 slowing of thought processes
4 ideas of unworthiness – tendency to deprecate self
5 early morning wakening (2–5 a.m.)
6 loss of appetite and decreased sex drive.

When the onset of depression occurs in middle age, and where no precipitating environmental factors can be isolated, the term *involutional melancholia* is usually employed.

The *circular manic-depressive reaction* involves dramatic swings of mood from the depths of depression to the heights of elation, although occasionally a transitional period of normality intervenes. Although, historically, both mania and depression were considered to be simply phases of the circular reaction which was presumed to be inevitable, it would now appear that only about 20 per cent of affective psychotics experience both ends of the mood continuum.

## Organic psychoses

In view of the very wide range of disorders grouped under this heading, and because of the non-psychological nature of the material, no attempt has been made here to provide a comprehensive account of the area. Instead the clinical signs common to most organic disorders are described and this is followed by a list of the various conditions.

*Definition.* This broad diagnostic category includes all those with severe personality disturbances which can be attributed, to a greater or lesser extent, to a disease or injury to the central nervous system. Although brain damage is very likely to bring about changes in behaviour, psychiatrists and psychologists are rarely involved unless neurotic or psychotic symptoms have been observed.

*Clinical picture.* The heterogeneous clinical pictures exhibited by neurological patients can be attributed to such factors as the extent and severity of the damage, locality of the pathology (see A2), and the pre-morbid personality of the individual. Nevertheless, certain patterns of symptomatology have been found to recur so frequently that the notion of the 'organic syndrome' has evolved.

It is customary to distinguish between the two sub-categories of *acute* and *chronic* brain damage. In the acute category are included all those physical disorders of a temporary nature such as those resulting from high fevers, hormonal disturbances, excessive drug intake or severe nutritional deficiencies. Since clinical psychologists are more involved with chronic disorders, where the damage is more severe and essentially irreversible, the acute disorders have been omitted from this discussion.

The following clinical signs are considered to be suggestive of brain damage:

1 memory disturbances – although distant events can still be recalled, recent memories are often badly preserved, and there is a tendency for the patient to 'confabulate' (i.e. invent facts) in order to fill these gaps;
2 affective changes – increase in emotional lability;
3 general intellectual impairment – less capable of abstract thinking, understanding new ideas, and making judgements
4 disorders of attention – easily distracted;
5 personality changes – the extent of these changes, while obviously related to the site of the injury, is thought to be very much a function of the stability of the pre-morbid personality. Furthermore, many of the changes themselves can be attributed to the concomitant stress as well as to the damage *per se*;
6 epileptic fits – damage to the brain in certain cases can disturb the rhythm of neural discharges and fits of a *petit mal* (mild) or *grand mal* (severe) nature may result.

Although the above are characteristic of all psychiatric organic states of the chronic variety, certain symptoms are more often associated with some types of disorders than with others. The following examples of common disorders, which can be distinguished on aetiological grounds, have fairly specific clinical pictures, although it should be emphasized that psychiatric symptoms alone would not enable one to make a definite diagnosis:

1 *Brain infections*. General paresis, or general paralysis of the insane as it is sometimes called, is the major psychiatric disorder caused by syphilis. During the early phase of the disease, the patient becomes careless and inattentive at work and at home, while failing to appreciate the severity of the situation. Formal clinical assessment typically reveals disorientation, memory defects and decline in intellectual abilities. Towards the terminal phase of the illness, he displays complete lack of interest in his surrounds, becomes increasingly inarticulate, and is generally unable to look after himself.
2 *Brain tumours*. The early symptoms of cerebral tumours are such physical symptoms as persistent headaches and vomit-

ing, and such psychological symptoms as apathy, memory impairment and general deterioration of intellectual functions. As the tumour progresses and the intracranial pressure increases, the symptoms become more marked and the patient eventually ends up in the vegetative state which is so characteristic of the terminal phase of all organic disorders.

3 *Brain injury*. Severe brain injury can cause symptoms which are associated with a diagnosis of psychosis. The car accident victim who has sustained damage to the brain is usually disoriented for time and place, lacking in initiative and unable to recollect anything about the accident.

4 *Degeneration of the nervous system*. There are a number of neurological degenerative diseases which give rise to psychiatric disturbances. In the case of senile dementia, the individual experiences difficulty in concentrating and comprehending new ideas. He seems generally less alert or interested in what is going on. Typically he reduces his social life and becomes more self-centred and preoccupied with his bodily functions. The other four major diseases in this category are Huntington's Chorea, Pick's Disease, Alzheimer's Disease and Parkinson's Disease. The clinical picture of these illnesses is very similar to that of senile dementia with the outstanding difference that these four can have their onset at any age.

### Mental retardation

The American Psychological Association (1970) defines mental retardation as 'primarily a psychosocial and psycho-educational problem – a deficit in adaptation to the demands and expectations of society evidenced by the individual's relative difficulty in learning, problem-solving, adapting to new situations, and abstract thinking.' (p. 267) There are two aspects of this definition which require further explanation:

The first concerns the use of the social criterion of 'deficit in adaptation' as opposed to the adoption of a cut-off point on an intelligence test (e.g. 70 IQ points). It is often extremely difficult to obtain a valid measure of intellectual functioning from patients who have some physical impairment such as spasticity or defective hearing. In addition the tests tend to underestimate the ability of those who have been educationally or socially deprived, or who originate from another culture.

The most important argument against the use of intelligence tests results on their own here is that many people with IQs of below 70 are able to support themselves and cope quite satisfactorily with the albeit limited demands of their environment. There would therefore seem to be little to be gained by labelling them subnormal.

The second point of note in this definition is the emphasis on the 'psychosocial and psychoeducational' (as opposed to 'medical') nature of this disorder. One reason for this is that although such biological factors as birth trauma, brain injury, thyroid deficiency (as in cretinism), and chromosomal abnormalities (as in mongolism) can bring about intellectual deficiency, in the vast majority of cases no physical cause can be found. Another reason is that, disregarding the nature of the aetiological factors, a social-cum-educational model has far more to offer in terms of actual management of the individual case than a medical one.

One point which is not clear from this definition is that the label of subnormality is generally used only in those cases where a low level of intellectual functioning has been apparent from an early age. Thus a person who scored below 70 IQ points and became unable to look after himself after experiencing injury to the brain in a car accident would be labelled 'brain damaged' rather than 'subnormal', despite possessing all the characteristics of members of this group. It could be argued that the question of labels in such a case is purely academic since the management programme most appropriate to his needs would be applied regardless of which diagnostic tag was applied. For present purposes it is sufficient to stress that the subnormality label implies a disorder involving the development of intellectual functioning rather than an inability to cope at a specific point in time.

One of the major problems in this field has been to devise a system for subdividing disorders characterized by low intellectual endowment. In the United Kingdom, the Mental Health Act of 1959 introduced the legal categories of 'subnormality' and 'severe subnormality' to replace the ill-defined terms of 'idiocy', 'imbecility' and 'feeble-mindedness'. A report of the British Psychological Society working party on subnormality (1963) recommended that an IQ of 55 (i.e. 3 standard deviations below the mean) should be used as the dividing line between the two groups. Although objective data is extremely useful in this complex field, the dangers of using psychological test scores on their own for classification purposes must be stressed once more. After all, as far as the individual case is concerned, the label is not merely a nominal designation, but a guide to teachers, parents and doctors as to how much should be expected from him. Thus an unwarranted classification of severe subnormality could lead to an individual being deprived of a lot of enjoyment and stimulation.

## Subnormality
*Definition.* Slater and Roth (1969) define subnormality as 'a state of arrested or incomplete development of mind (not amounting to severe subnormality) which includes subnormality of intelligence and is of a nature and degree which requires or is susceptible to medical treatment or other special care or training of the patient'. This can be criticized on account of the response to treatment criterion which is tantamount to suggesting that a diagnosis can only be made with confidence after treatment has been attempted. If this is the case then it would be argued that the diagnostic label is of little value. The emphasis on 'medical' treatment is something which would not meet with universal approval.

*Clinical picture.* As well as simply being of low intelligence, there are certain other aspects of psychological functioning which are seen to be characteristic of the subnormal:

1 lack of curiosity and interest in surrounds
2 inability to use abstract concepts
3 slow to respond to stimulation despite intact senses
4 habit-bound – well-learned sequences of behaviour used in inappropriate settings
5 no primary disturbance of memory – obviously in view of their low intelligence they do not retain things so well
6 normal affective responses – despite crudity of expression, emotions seem undisturbed
7 speech poorly articulated and lacking in expression
8 inadequate muscular co-ordination

## Severe subnormality
*Definition.* This has been defined as 'a state of arrested or incomplete development of mind which includes subnormality of intelligence and is of such a nature or degree that the patient is incapable of leading an independent life' (Slater and Roth, 1969).

*Clinical picture.* Those classified as severly abnormal possess many of the features described above, but there are three symptoms which are considered to be particularly associated with severe subnormality:

1 marked physical abnormalities – squints, paralyses and mis-shapen heads etc
2 emotionally infantile – feelings of sorrow or joy suddenly aroused and just as quickly banished
3 restless and distractible – constant need of stimulation

### Summary and conclusions

In this chapter, the five categories of psychiatric disorders were presented along with definitions and descriptions of the most common sub-types in each case. It was stressed at the beginning that this framework is very much the backbone of the medically-oriented approach to psychological disorders. Such a list of illnesses, with associated diagnostic signs and symptoms, is the *sine qua non* of the medical model. In the absence of such a system, it would be impossible to carry out experimentation to determine common aetiological factors, prognostic signs and treatment efficacies. Consequently both the medical scientists who are researching in this area, and the practising clinician who wants to know which pills to give to which patient, have a lot invested in this system.

In the next few chapters, evidence is supplied in order to demonstrate that, despite its longevity, the whole structure of traditional psychiatry is far less sound than it appears. The implications of this for the medical model are considered.

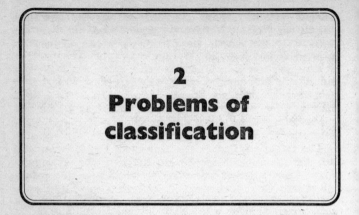

# 2
# Problems of classification

Although at first sight the classification system described in the previous chapter would seem to provide the clinician with a useful framework within which to view his patients, on closer inspection the picture is somewhat less satisfactory. Criticisms of the system range from Foulds' suggestion (1955) that the current system requires some minor refinements, to Rogers' view (1965) that all classification systems in this field are not only useless but can actually be obstructive where therapy is concerned. Since the issues involved are quite distinct, both these points of view are presented separately in this chapter. Although many of the classification critics are, not surprisingly, psychologists, only the views of dissenters from within the ranks of psychiatry itself are considered here. The positions taken on these issues by some of the more influential psychologists are dealt with in some depth in the second section.

*Criticisms of the present system*
The four major criticisms of the neo-Kraepelinian classifications are that the categories lack independence, the principles underlying them are diverse, they are too heterogeneous, and the reliability (i.e. degree of consistency) and validity (i.e. degree of correctness) of diagnoses are too low to be of any value.

Lack of independence between classes: For a classification system to be useful, it should provide some guidance as to the boundaries between neighbouring groups. If such dividing lines cannot be specified then the assumption that specific categories actually exist is very much open to question. It [?] has already been suggested that psychiatrists, as a rule, find it difficult to distinguish between reactive and endogenous depression, and between the various types of schizophrenia. It could, of course, be argued in defence that certain of these sub-groups were created erroneously and that proof of their non-existence does not actually threaten the whole system. However, for the system to be worthwhile it should at least provide clear guidelines for distinguishing between such major categories as normality, neurosis and psychosis.

The presumed fundamental distinctions between normality and the psychopathologies in general have proved tantalizingly elusive for those committed to the classification system. All of the symptoms associated with each of the disorders are experienced to a greater or lesser extent by all of us at some time or other. We all have panic attacks, low moods and certain rituals which we feel compelled to carry out in a similar manner to the neurotic. We break the speed limit, drink and drive, and fiddle expense accounts with the nonchalance supposed to be characteristic of the psychopath. We have exaggerated feelings of our own importance, hide our emotions, and have problems keeping to the point of a discussion as the psychotic does. The difference between the normal and the clinically abnormal is seen to lie in the degree of persistence of the symptoms which the neurotic complains of and of the signs demonstrated by the psychotic.

In the final analysis, therefore, clinical intuition is used to determine whether the individual is to be regarded as normal or abnormal. The subjective nature of this criterion would suggest that there is a greater likelihood of the patient being described as 'sick' if his experiences and behaviour do not closely resemble those of the psychiatrist who is assessing him. Thus many of the anti-psychiatry pressure groups feel strongly that the middle-class values of the psychiatrist determine to a large extent the sort of people who are labelled 'mad' in this country (see F8). We shall return to the question of values at a later stage, but it is important to emphasize here that the distinction between normality and abnormality is by no means clear.

A somewhat disturbing investigation, conducted by Rosenhahn (1973), clearly illustrates this point. Eight apparently 'normal' people (a psychology student, three psychologists, a paediatrician, a psychiatrist, a painter and a housewife) went to the admissions offices of various assorted mental hospitals and complained of hearing voices. The only falsification which took place concerned the report of this symptom and the name and occupation of the participants. Despite the fact that they did not fabricate any additional symptoms or peculiarities in their life histories and circumstances, the eight pseudo-patients were taken into hospital for treatment. As soon as they had been admitted, they all stopped simulating symptoms and engaged in their ordinary behaviour. The fears of many that they would be immediately detected as frauds at this point turned out to have no foundation. In fact their true clinical status was never suspected at any stage and all were eventually discharged with a diagnosis of schizophrenia 'in remission'. The obvious conclusion to be drawn from this study is that it is certainly not outside the bounds of possibility for psychiatrists to diagnose 'sane' people as 'insane'.

The failure to detect sanity is an example of a Type Two error, i.e. a false positive (see A8), and supports the general policy in medicine that 'it is better to be safe than sorry'. To see if the bias was purely in this direction, a second experiment was carried out by the same author. Here he attempted to determine the likelihood of psychiatrists committing a Type One error (i.e. a false negative) by labelling 'sick' people 'healthy'. This study involved simply informing members of a teaching hospital of the above findings and warning them that some pseudo-patients would be attempting to gain entry during a particular three-month period. Each member of staff was asked to rate every new patient as to the likelihood of his being an impostor. Of the 193 patients who were admitted during the experimental period, forty-one were confidently alleged to be pseudo-patients by at least one member of staff, twenty-three were regarded suspiciously by at least one psychiatrist, and nineteen were considered to be suspect by one psychiatrist and one other person. The fact that no pseudo-patients actually presented themselves would suggest that it is possible for the 'insane' to be regarded as 'sane' by trained psychiatric staff.

Rosenhahn spells out the implications of his findings, that psychiatrists cannot clearly distinguish the 'sane' from the 'insane' by posing the following rhetorical questions:

How many people, one wonders, are sane but not recognized as such in our psychiatric institutions? How many have feigned insanity in order to avoid the criminal consequences of their behaviour, and, conversely, how many would rather stand trial than live interminably in a psychiatric hospital but are wrongly thought to be mentally ill? How many have been stigmatized by well-intentioned, but nevertheless erroneous, diagnoses?

Although the ambiguous nature of the normality/abnormality boundary is a severe limitation, the classification scheme would still be regarded as useful should the various disorders, presumed to be encompassed by it, be seen to be relatively distinct entities. This is by no means the case however. Even so far as the two major types of disorders – the neuroses and the psychoses – are concerned, there is little agreement as to the precise nature of the dividing line between them. Various suggestions have been made but there is no single criterion which, by itself, is sufficient to enable the clinician to make a distinction between the two without fear of contradiction.

One of the most commonly proposed divisions is that neurotics have some awareness of their problems whereas psychotics do not. However, as was seen, one feature of hysteria is 'la belle indifférence' or complete lack of concern about the symptoms. Similarly, psychopaths rarely feel that they are suffering from a 'personality defect' which requires treatment. On the other hand it is by no means unknown for people who have been diagnosed as psychotic to be concerned and unhappy about their mental state.

Another proposed distinction which has been put forward is that the psychotic tends to engage in activities which can endanger his life or the lives of others, whereas the neurotic can look after himself without supervision. This dividing line does not hold up altogether because those neurotics with anorexia nervosa will starve themselves to death unless treated. Similarly, depressives may commit suicide as a result of excessive stress in the environment. On the other hand there are many patients who have been diagnosed psychotic who are quite capable of looking after themselves and keeping out of danger.

Once again the psychiatrist has to use his subjective impression as to whether the behaviour is just an exaggerated form of normal behaviour or whether it is qualitatively distinct. What is particularly distressing here is that the decision he makes on such limited knowledge has all sorts of repercussions for the individual. If he is labelled neurotic then he will receive sympathy from his family and employers, whereas if he is awarded a diagnosis of psychotic, then he will be very likely hospitalized and stigmatized, perhaps for the rest of his life.

Thomas Szasz (1966), the outspoken critic of the medical model, has this to say about classification:

> All discussion of the problem of classification in psychiatry rests on the fundamental premise: that there exists in nature abnormal mental conditions or forms of behaviour, that it is scientifically worthwhile and morally meritorious to place persons suffering from these conditions, or displaying such behaviour, into appropriately named categories. (p. 127)

Szasz is not impressed by the evidence supporting such an assumption.

*Diversity of classification principles*

One fundamental rule concerning classification systems is that the type of material used to define the attributes of the various categories should be consistent throughout. If this is not the case then all sorts of conceptual problems arise. Thus it would be nonsensical to state that the difference between a dog and a chicken is that the dog has four legs whereas a chicken began life as an egg.

In the psychiatric classification system, however, although symptoms are generally used to determine diagnosis, occasions arise when information about aetiology or response to treatment is considered to be more significant than details of the clinical picture. Thus, for instance, if a person is diagnosed as schizophrenic on the basis of his presenting signs and symptoms, and it is later discovered that he had received some form of brain surgery, then it is highly unlikely that the original label will be kept. In other words, strong aetiological data is regarded as superior to clinical data. Similarly, if someone who has been originally diagnosed as psychotic makes a rapid recovery, there is a tendency to conclude that he must really have been suffering from a personality disorder all the time. In this latter case, the naming game is clearly a waste of time since the whole object of the exercise is to enable the clinician to predict the course of the disorder and to make a decision regarding therapy. A retrospective label is merely a piece of redundant information.

To summarize this point, since neither clinical nor aetiological data are sufficiently unambiguous to define the attributes of a particular class, it can be argued that this system of categorization is of very dubious value.

*Homogeneity*

In any classification system there must be some sort of common thread running through the sub-groups of a particular category. There may, of course, be a wide range of attributes within a category, but for it to be seen to exist it is essential that each of the members of the sub-category should possess one or two fundamental characteristics in common.

The psychiatric system has been widely criticized on these grounds. For instance Wittenborn (1951) found that individuals who shared a common diagnosis differed greatly from each other in terms of the symptom patterns which had been previously isolated using a statistical technique based on correlations called *factor analysis* (see F1). He concluded from these findings that the traditional diagnostic groups were therefore not homogeneous. This interpretation of the results has been challenged by Zigler and Phillips (1961) on the grounds that the assumption that data from factor analysis is necessarily superior to clinical data is open to question. The information gleaned from a sophisticated statistical analysis gives the impression of being more valid but it has its limitations in that the type of factors which emerge is very much a function of the sort of material which is put in. Zigler and Phillips argue this case as follows:

> The merit accruing through the greater rigor of factor analysis may be outweighed by the limitations imposed in employing a restricted group of symptoms and a particular sample of patients. Thus the factor analyst cannot claim that the class-defining symptom pattern he has derived is a standard of homogeneity against which classes within another scheme can be evaluated. (p. 607)

The homogeneity argument has very often been raised specifically in relation to the category of schizophrenia. Some psychiatrists have argued that patients whose 'illness' is characterized mainly by delusional thinking should be grouped in the separate category of 'paranoid psychosis', on the grounds that the onset tends to occur later in life, deterioration rarely takes place, and the patients tend to be of above average intelligence. Others, however, feel that they have a sufficient number of features in common for them to be categorized similarly. More significantly, Bannister (1968) argues that it is possible for one person to have some of the primary symptoms of schizophrenia, another person to have the remaining ones, and for them both to be labelled schizophrenic despite the fact that they have no symptoms in common. Thus although schizophrenia has turned out to be very much the 'Achilles' heel' of psychiatry, it would appear very significant that, almost a hundred years after Kraepelin first introduced his syndromes into psychological medicine, there should be such lack of agreement as to whether there are sufficient common features among the basic types for them to be usefully bracketed together.

The elusiveness of patients who fit neatly into one or other of the Kraepelinian pigeon-holes is perhaps most clearly illustrated by reference to the current practice of employing composite diagnostic labels. Thus many patients are described as having, say, 'a schizo-affective disorder in a borderline subnormal with psychopathic tendencies', or as suffering from 'chronic depression with paranoid features in a basically hysterical personality'. Thus reality has, in effect, led to persistent violations of the artificial class boundaries. Following on from this, I must confess to having felt some sympathy for those of my psychiatric colleagues who have had, as a duty, to find a 'typical' manic-depressive or schizophrenic, out of their hundreds of patients, to use for teaching purposes. Cases which correspond to the classic types seem to appear remarkably infrequently. The symptoms of the individual patient are generally so idiosyncratic as to defy simple categorization. Thus homogeneity within categories, which is such an important property of all classification systems, would seem to be significantly lacking so far as the traditional psychiatric schema is concerned.

*Reliability and validity*
For a measuring instrument to be considered to be of value, it must be shown to be both reliable and valid. In other words it should produce the same sort of result each time and it should measure what it sets out to measure (see D3, E2). A glance at the history of psychometrics reveals that an enormous number of IQ and personality tests have been discarded because they fail to meet these requirements. Psychiatric classification can be regarded as a form of assessment and, although it constitutes a nominal (i.e. non-numerical) scale (see A8), it can still be subjected to rigorous scientific investigation.

The *validity* question lies at the heart of all criticisms levied against the psychiatric classification system. If the particular label does not permit the psychiatrist to make a prediction about aetiology, prognosis or response to treatment, then it is an invalid form of assessment and should be regarded, at best, simply as a useful language for facilitating communication between clinicians. Critics, such as Kanfer and Phillips (1970) report that the relationship between diagnosis on the one hand and response to treatment on the other is, in fact, a very tenuous one. Thus even if a unitary diagnostic label can be arrived at, this generally provides relatively little information as to the precise nature of the treatment, whether physical or psychological, the individual patient should receive. As a rule, therapy tends to be carried out on a fairly ad hoc basis, with each clinician employing his own favoured 'menus' of therapies. Diagnosis would therefore seem to provide merely a redundant descriptive tag, rather than a set of guidelines for action.

Much more work has been carried out into the *reliability* of psychiatric diagnosis. For the system to be useful, even as an aid to communication, it is important that there is some agreement as to what the terms actually mean. Once again, however, the evidence does not favour the continued use of psychiatric diagnosis even in this limited capacity. Schmidt and Fonda (1956), for instance, arranged for two psychiatrists to diagnose 426 patients using the official diagnostic categories which were currently employed at that time. Although there was 92 per cent, 80 per cent and 71 per cent agreement on the use of organic, psychotic and characterological (i.e. neurotic plus personality disorder) categories respectively, the reliability was much lower where specific diagnostic categories were concerned. For instance, there was only 41 per cent agreement on mental deficiency and 51 per cent on schizophrenia. Other studies, using different methodologies, have produced similar results. Thus Beck (1962) presented essentially identical data to clinicians on two different occasions and found that they tended to use different diagnoses. Investigations using the more orthodox test/re-test methodology, in which raters assess the same person on two separate occasions, have also demonstrated the low reliability of diagnosis.

These studies have, however, been widely criticized (e.g. Buss, 1966) on several grounds. In the first place it is claimed that the diagnosticians were relatively inexperienced. In the second place the lack of consistency is attributed to differences in training. The artificiality of the whole situation is a third argument which as been raised against this collection of studies. Finally the fact that the clinicians were receiving unequal amounts of information from each patient has also

45

been put forward as an explanation of the low agreement. Certainly the better controlled studies (e.g. Wilson and Meyer, 1962) have produced more encouraging results for supporters of the system.

The great bulk of the evidence would, however, suggest that although there is high agreement where the major categories are concerned, there are marked differences of opinion between clinicians concerning the use of more specific categories. Furthermore the individual clinician does not seem to be too consistent in the way he uses the various categories. Thus, even if its functions are restricted to those of a formal language, the classification scheme does not emerge with much credit.

There are, however, many psychologists who feel that, despite these various inadequacies, the Kraepelinian system still has a lot to offer. Thus Meehl (1959) defends the use of psychiatric diagnosis as follows: 'There is a sufficient amount of aetiological and prognostic homogeneity among patients belonging to a given diagnostic group, so that the assignment of a patient to his group has probability implications which it is clinically unsound to ignore.' (p. 103)

His main counter-argument to the reliability criticism is that the fact that people do not use the system correctly is a reflection on their lack of skills rather than on the system itself. However, since the fully-trained psychiatrists who were used in these experiments were generally unable to agree as to which pigeon-hole a patient should be placed in, one could be forgiven for continuing to wonder whether such compartments really are justified at all.

*Criticisms of all classification systems*
Although the Kraepelinian system has its problems, it does not follow from this that there is no place for a classification system in psychiatry. Nomothetic theorists, such as Cattell and Eysenck, feel that a classification system is essential if the disciplines of psychiatry and clinical psychology are to be regarded as scientific. Eysenck (1960) argues his case as follows: 'Before we can reasonably be asked to look for the cause of a particular dysfunction or disorder, we must have isolated, however crudely, the dysfunction or disorder in question, and we must be able to recognize it and differentiate it from other syndromes.' (p. 1)

Brendan Maher (1970), a stout defender of the experimental approach to psychopathology, makes a similar point:

Even though we have seen that descriptive diagnosis may be criticized as misleading when it is allowed to substitute for aetiological diagnosis, we should note that it serves an important purpose in the early study of natural phenomena. Before we can begin to search effectively for the origins of a specific pattern of events, we must have established a reasonably good definition of the pattern and have been assured that it tends to occur with some internal regularity. (p. 33)

Clearly supporters of the experimental approach have a lot invested in the assumption that such categories of abnormal behaviour do in fact exist. There are, however, many who would take an idiographic viewpoint and claim that each individual is totally unique. There are still others who would claim that even if there is some regularity in this field, there is little to be gained by such a labelling exercise. Within the field of orthodox psychiatry, two highly influential figures, who had little regard for classification systems while supporting the notion of mental illness, stand out in particular. They are Adolf Meyer, the so-called 'dean of American psychiatry', and Sigmund Freud, the 'father of psychoanalysis'.

## Meyer's school of psychobiology

Meyer's psychobiological approach places its emphasis on regarding the patient as a unique individual (see D1), who cannot be broken down into lists of symptoms or categorized alongside others with superficially similar clinical pictures. He rebelled against the Cartesian dualistic philosophy which formed the basis of German psychiatry, and instead proposed that biological, psychological and social factors should be regarded as interacting together to produce mental illnesses. Following on from this, he argued that each individual should be studied in great detail so that the various background causes of the psychobiological reaction could be elicited and appropriate treatment programmes subsequently designed exclusively for him.

On the treatment side, because of his belief in the uniqueness of the individual, he found no place, as such, for electroconvulsive therapy (ECT), i.e. shock treatment for depressives, or insulin therapy in his system, because they were designed to be applied to particular classes of persons. However his own particular psychotherapeutic approach, known as 'personality analysis' did not prove particularly successful and has failed to stand the test of time. The fact that one of the classic commentaries on his work is entitled *The Common-sense Psychiatry of Adolf Meyer* (Lief, 1948) is an indication of the lack of sophistication and depth in his approach.

Thus although in many ways his line of thinking is in keeping with many contemporary 'whole person' views in medicine, the absence of a distinct and efficacious brand of therapy has meant that he is now regarded mainly as a figure of great historical importance only.

*Freud's school of psychoanalysis*
The school of psychoanalysis, which maintains that all psychological disturbances are caused by unconscious processes, was founded by Sigmund Freud. Freud shared with Meyer the view that detailed analysis of the individual's life history was essential for a full understanding of his problems. His model, however, was far more systematic than the American's and provided a framework within which the interrelationships of biological, psychological, sociological and anthropological factors in personality development and human functioning could be viewed (see D3).

It is argued by Szasz that one of the reasons why Freud made such major contributions was because 'he was not fettered in making his observations in a single situation with limited techniques' (Szasz, 1957, p. 167). Although he made use of the diagnostic terms introduced by Kraepelin and others, he employed them very freely and later summaries of his most celebrated cases have involved extensive re-labelling. It would appear, therefore, that Freud used the diagnostic tags as linguistic conveniences rather than as integral parts of his theories. He was far more concerned to understand the patient's problems in terms of his life context rather than to place him into a clinical grouping.

Although neo-Freudians have tended to make more use of these categories in order to organize their thinking more clearly, there has always been a tendency in the psychoanalytic literature to regard the individual as an object of inquiry in his own right, rather than as a member of a typology. Traditionalists like Slater and Roth (1969) sound incredulous that 'many analysts find it difficult to understand that there are differences between the normal and the diseased, between the neurotic and the psychotic, or between reactive and endogenous disorders' (p. 15).

The psychoanalytic approach will be considered in detail in Part Two. It is sufficient to emphasize here that, although the medical notion that the presenting problems are merely symptoms of underlying pathology is a fundamental assumption made by analysts, they differ from organic practitioners in that they tend to concentrate on the individual rather than on the disorders.

## Summary and conclusions

As has been shown, there are many problems associated with the current classification system in psychiatry. It had been assumed by Kraepelin and his supporters that it should prove possible in time to produce a list of the various illnesses with their associated symptoms. However, despite repeated modifications, improved training facilities and clear-cut guidelines from national and international institutions, the progress towards this goal has been modest. Admittedly there is now general agreement as to when the major categories of neurosis, functional psychosis and organic psychosis should be used, but these categories are so heterogeneous as to provide only a bare minimum of information. Diagnosis at a more detailed level would be of far more value to the clinician, but unfortunately reliability of assessment, as far as such sub-classes are concerned, is far from impressive.

Some psychiatrists have argued that even if there were greater agreement in assigning patients to categories, this would contribute relatively little to the understanding and treatment of the individual case. They argue that the individual is absolutely unique and that, despite any similarities that might exist between himself and others, the therapeutic approach which is adopted should be tailor-made for him alone. These notions will be explored further in the second section.

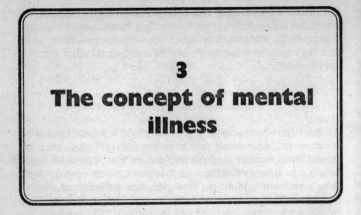

# 3
# The concept of mental illness

As has already been indicated in the introduction, the notion of mental illness is no more a proven fact than that of spiritual possession (see F1 and F8). It is merely the cornerstone of a working hypothesis which was set up in order to determine to what extent the medical model could explain and provide remedies for psychological disturbances. Despite the fact that relatively little evidence has been acquired over the past century to support the continued use of this concept, the assumption that diseases of the mind actually exist is still widely accepted by both medical practitioners and lay people alike. One of the many reasons (see introduction) why the medical model is still very much in vogue is because of certain dramatic contributions which it made, or at least appeared to have made, in its early days. Its currently high reputation rests heavily on these early advances. It is useful to divide these contributions into three categories:

1. From a *humanitarian* point of view, the medical model, once and for all, dispelled all of the medieval torturous interventions, such as exorcism and witch-hunting. It should be emphasized, however, that Pinel and his contemporaries were the first to advocate the removal of chains and other restraining devices, and it would be fallacious to award all the credit for this to Medicine. It could in fact be argued that the moral therapists treated the inmates with more kindness and consideration than the medical practitioners who followed. Zilboorg and Henry (1941), for instance, observe that the approach of Kraepelin was, at the same time, both humane

50

and inhuman. In other words he was interested in man but not in men.

One important contribution here is undoubtedly the tremendous advances achieved by pharmacologists in the 1950s, culminating in the wide range of *psychotropic* drugs (i.e. drugs which act directly on psychological processes) which are now available. Without them, many people who are able to play an active role in the community would find themselves unable to cope. Many, however, would argue against the 'curative' effects of these drugs, and claim that what has happened in the last twenty years is that pharmacological straitjackets have been substituted for those of the more mechanical variety. As a recent patient of mine commented, 'they keep you afloat, but they don't teach you how to swim'. Be this as it may, they have certainly helped to achieve Pinel's great ambition of keeping the psychologically disturbed in the community.

2. From a *scientific* viewpoint, the medical model produced a classification system which has led to extensive research into the aetiology, prognosis and treatments of the various kinds of psychological disturbances. However, the bulk of this research has added very little to our understanding of human problems and, as has been shown earlier, even the very existence of these disease entities is far from being generally accepted.

3. From the standpoint of *medicine*, perhaps the greatest contribution has been that various mental disorders have been found to be associated with brain pathology. These early findings suggested to the pioneering psychiatrists of the last century that the organic bases of all psychological problems would be discovered in time. At this stage it would appear that this early optimism was unfounded. Even with the so-called organic psychoses, there are problems in that many people with extensive brain damage demonstrate few clinical signs, whereas gross mental impairment can occur with patients whose injury has been relatively slight. Thus obviously psychological factors are very important even in the apparently undisputed medical areas.

### 'Health' and 'illness' in medicine and psychiatry

The gradual realization that the contributions of the medical model to the understanding of psychological disturbances has been somewhat meagre, has led to widespread criticism of the concepts of mental health and illness (see F1). The term illness has been defined as 'any marked deviation, physical, mental, or behavioral, from normally desirable standards of structural and functional integrity' (Ausubel, 1961, p. 71). It is the ambiguous nature of these 'standards' and 'deviations' in the psychiatric field which has led to the current state of unrest.

*Health.* In physical medicine, there is little dispute as to the precise nature of health. As Szasz (1960) points out, 'the norm is the structural and functional integrity of the human body' (p. 115). In other words, if no abnormalities are present, the organism is considered to be in good health. The physician is not required to make a moral or philosophical decision when declaring someone to be healthy because 'what health is can be stated in anatomical and physical terms' (Szasz, ibid). True, health is a highly desirable state, but values, as such, are not involved when determining whether someone is healthy or otherwise. What makes the situation particularly straightforward here is that the ideal and statistical norms are roughly equivalent. In other words, the majority of people correspond closely to the desired state of affairs.

In psychiatry, the notion of health is far less clearcut. Although organic psychiatrists might maintain that mental health is merely the absence of signs, many others would argue that this medical analogy does not go far enough and that additional criteria are required. For example, the social psychologist, Marie Jahoda, has emphasized the positive striving aspects of mentally healthy behaviour. For her, the healthy person should be actively engaged in adapting to his environment, his personality should be fully intact despite the flexibility of his adaptive behaviour, and his perception of the world, and of himself, should not be distorted by motivational factors (Jahoda, 1958).

Similarly, Maslow stresses the positive nature of mental health and equates this state with the on-going process of what he calls 'self-actualization'. He defines this as the 'full use and exploration of talents, capacities, potentialities' (Maslow, 1970, p. 150). It comprises the following ten components:

1 efficient perception of reality
2 acceptance of self and others
3 spontaneity, simplicity, and naturalness
4 quality for detachment
5 the need for privacy

6 peak experience (i.e. non-self-centred state of perfection achieved without striving)
7 problem centring
8 autonomy
9 feelings for mankind
10 creativeness

While few would dispute that these are laudable attributes to possess, the problem, so far as adopting them as criteria for mental health is concerned, is that the majority of the population would therefore have to be considered to be maladjusted. In other words, so far as Jahoda and Maslow are concerned, the ideal and statistical norms are highly discrepant. This, as we have seen, is very different from the situation in physical medicine.

*Illness.* Leaving aside these philosophical issues for the moment, it is interesting to compare the ways in which organic psychiatrists and physicians reach decisions regarding the diagnosis of a disease. In both branches of medicine, use is made of both *signs* (i.e. results of objective tests) and *symptoms* (i.e. subjective reports of distress) when determining, in the first place, whether a disorder is present and, if the answer is in the affirmative, the specific type of disorder the person is suffering from. There are however striking differences in the nature of these indicators and in the ways they are used in physical medicine and psychiatry. For the purposes of this discussion, the terms 'sign' and 'symptom' will be used in accordance with their traditional medical meanings, as defined above.

*Signs.* In physical medicine there are 'hard' signs, such as blood tests and X-rays which, while certainly not free from the possibility of misinterpretation, are considered to be fairly reliable measures. There are also 'soft' signs such as the 'prod' administered by the family doctor in order to determine whether a particular part of the body is tender or not. Because of the relatively unstandardized procedures involved in the latter case, more reliance tends to be placed on laboratory test results.

Similarly in psychiatry there are two groups of signs which correspond to the 'hard' and 'soft' categories described above. Psychometric test results, being objective data collected under standardized conditions, are the equivalent of the laboratory tests in physical medicine. 'Soft' signs in psychiatry include the clinical impression which the psychiatrist has of the patient, after observing his behaviour in an unstructured sort of way in an interview or on the ward. The status of the two types of test is quite the reverse in psychiatry. Psychological tests have not proved so capable of distinguishing between pathological conditions as their physical counterparts (see Ch. 4). Consequently the less standardized signs are considered to carry more weight in the majority of cases.

In physical medicine, although information about signs and symptoms is usually collated when diagnostic decisions are being made, signs are generally regarded as constituting superior data to symptomatology. Thus if the blood test indicates an abnormality, then a disorder is diagnosed, even if the patient fails to report any feelings of discomfort. This is also the case in psychiatry, at least so far as psychotic disorders are concerned. So if the patient exhibits thought disorder or flatness of affect he will be regarded as 'ill' even though he denies experiencing distress. Thus, in cases of psychosis, the psychiatrist behaves very much like his counterpart in physical medicine in paying more attention to signs than to the patient's report.

There is however one important difference between the nature of signs in psychiatry and in general medicine. Whereas, in the case of the latter, statistical abnormality is virtually synonymous with pathology (e.g. raised blood pressure and hypertension), this is far from being the case in psychiatry. Thus an individual can exhibit very unusual behaviour and not be declared 'mad' (e.g. the genius; eccentric entertainer). In other words, statistical data is always considered alongside evaluative judgements where mental illness is concerned.

It follows from this that it is possible to be labelled 'sick' in one country and 'well' in another. Thus western psychiatrists have been very concerned recently that psychiatrists in eastern European countries have apparently been declaring Communist dissenters to be 'mad'. Similarly, at least until recently, western psychiatrists have been labelling homosexuals as 'sick', while there are communities throughout the world where homosexuality is regarded as at least as natural a form of behaviour as heterosexuality. Also, a daily amount of alcoholic consumption which is regarded as pathological in one country may be regarded as perfectly acceptable in another. This is in sharp contrast to the situation in physical medicine where sociocultural values play no part in determining the presence of a disease or the severity of a disorder. The clinical signs of tuberculosis are identical in Japan, England and Iceland.

There are even occasions in psychiatry where evaluative factors are considered to be *more* important than the frequency of occurrence of the behaviour in the general population. Masters and Johnson (1970) claim that some 50 per cent of American marriages suffer from sexual dysfunction of one kind or another. With the obvious exception of epidemics, such a situation does not occur in physical medicine.

To summarize, therefore, in general medicine a marked deviation from the statistical norm is normally sufficient to indicate the presence of a disorder. In psychiatry, social norms and values are important and can even be of greater significance than the degree to which the behaviour is unusual.

*Symptoms.* As stated above, the physician is generally unimpressed by symptoms in the absence of signs. As a rule, if the patient reports distress, and all investigations prove negative, then he is likely to be classified as physically well. No medical treatment will be administered in such cases. One obvious exception is in the case of headaches, where the general practitioner may prescribe medication purely on the basis of reported symptoms. By and large, however, the physician diagnoses and treats on the basis of signs.

The psychiatrist, on the other hand, finds himself in many cases working with sign-free, symptomatic problems. A large proportion of his time is spent treating people who *feel* tense, confused or unhappy, and who do not behave abnormally or deviate significantly from psychometric norms. Thus, unlike his physician colleagues, the psychiatrist rarely hesitates from prescribing medication for mere symptoms. There are however problems associated with such an uncritical acceptance of personal distress as an indication of illness:

1. The individual has his own ideas as to how much suffering is 'normal' and, if he grossly underestimates this, then he might wrongly classify himself as being 'abnormal'. The clinician, being unaware of his distortion of the norms, accepts his view of things and treats him accordingly. By so doing, he may be confirming the patient's belief that he does have a real problem. One possible offshoot of this is that a friend of the patient may reason that he is under just as much pressure and seek similar help. This sort of 'modelling' is

possibly one of the factors contributing to the increasingly heavy use of tranquillizers in our society.

2. Grief following the loss of a loved one and bitterness following rejection can be seen to be 'normal' reactions to environmental stress and should not necessarily be regarded as pathological responses. Once more, by regarding symptoms as indications of illness the practitioner can unwittingly help to confirm the individual's mistaken view that he is mentally unstable, with all the ensuing legal and social implications.

Those who defend the heavy reliance on symptoms in psychiatry would claim that, in the absence of sophisticated tests, the clinician *has* to rely on the information provided by the patient. The important question here is whether it is believed that objective instruments will ever be developed which are considered to be as powerful indicators of pathology as, say, blood tests. If the answer to this question is 'no', (and at this point in time there are a few grounds for optimism in this regard) then one has to acknowledge the fact that the status of symptoms in psychiatry and medicine is highly discrepant. Once again the illness analogy in relation to psychological problems would appear to be a weak one.

## The views of Thomas Szasz

No critical discussion of the mental illness concept would be complete without reference to the veteran campaigner for its abolition, Thomas Szasz. In his classic paper, 'The Myth of Mental Illness', Szasz (1960) puts forward three basic propositions to support his provocative title:

1. He begins by arguing that the notion of mental illness is mainly supported by the findings that organic conditions can lead to psychological disturbances. It is assumed by many, he claims, that a physical cause will be found for all such disturbances. Should this be the case, he argues, then those disorders should be regarded as neurological rather than mentalistic. In his own words, 'I have tried to show that for those who regard mental symptoms as signs of brain disease, the concept of mental illness is unnecessary and misleading. For what they mean is that people so labelled suffer from diseases of the brain; and, if that is what they mean, it would seem better for the sake of charity to say that and not something else' (p. 114).

2. His second point concerns the fact that evaluation is involved in the case of mental illness but not of physical ill-

ness. This issue has been discussed above and therefore will only be mentioned briefly here. Szasz summarizes the position as follows: 'The notion of mental symptom is therefore inextricably tied to the *social* (including *ethical*) *context* in which it is made in much the same way as the notion of bodily symptom is tied to an *anatomical* and *genetic context*' (p. 114).

3. In place of the concept of mental illness, he suggests the more nebulous one of 'problems in living'. It is important to emphasize that he is not concerned to develop an alternative model to the medical one, but merely to indicate the shortcomings of the latter. Thus:

> I do not intend to offer a new conception of 'psychiatric illness' nor a new form of 'therapy'. My aim is more modest yet also more ambitious. It is to suggest that the phenomena now called mental illnesses be looked at afresh and more simply, that they be removed from the category of illnesses, and that they be regarded as the expressions of man's struggle with the problem of *how* he should live. (p. 117)

Despite a tendency to overstate the somaticists' case, there is no doubt that the provocative and challenging writings of Szasz have gone a long way towards dispelling the feelings of complacency regarding the illness notion, which were apparent particularly after the psychopharmacological breakthroughs of the 1950s. If he has achieved little else, he has at least reminded psychiatrists throughout the world that the medical model is adhered to because it provides a particular working hypothesis in a complex area rather than because it possesses 'the truth'. Due to the fact that he refused to suggest any guidelines for the future, Szasz will just be remembered as the first and most energetic critic of the place of psychiatry within medicine.

## The social implications of mental illness

That society itself is merely paying lip-service to the notion of mental illness is clearly demonstrated by the fact that the individual who visits a psychiatrist is generally not simply regarded as 'sick' by his friends and acquaintances. He is likely to be either scorned or feared by these people in a way which he would not should he be suffering from pneumonia or a broken leg. Thus Elinson *et al.* (1967), who carried out a survey into society's attitudes to psychiatric disorders, conclude that 'the stigma that traditionally has been attached to mental illness still lingers in the minds of many people'. A more recent investigation carried out by Sarbin and Mancuso (1970) produced similar results.

Thus, essentially, classifying a person as mentally ill is tantamount to declaring him to be a social outcast. It is generally assumed that people never really recover from mental illnesses as they do from physical ones. For instance, the majority of application forms devised by insurance companies contain the question 'Have you *ever* suffered from mental illness of any kind?' As Sarbin (1967) points out, 'It is as if the mental state were capable of disguising the person as healthy, although the underlying mental illness remains in a dormant or latent state' (p. 451). He goes on from this to argue that this prejudice against those who have received psychiatric treatment tends to operate as a 'self-fulfilling prophecy'. By treating someone as not being capable of taking on responsibilities, it is highly likely that he will, in fact, fail to do so, thus confirming the initial hypothesis. There are two important aspects concerning the stigma of mental illness which require some elaboration here.

In the first place, it is disturbing to realize that the vague notions outlined above regarding the nature of mental illness are actually being applied to render people, to a certain extent, social outcasts. Furthermore, it will be recalled that a psychiatric diagnosis requires a judgement based on a set of values. According to an early writer on this topic (Davis, 1938), this is generally taken to be the middle-class protestant ethic (i.e. democratic, worldly, ascetic, individualistic, rationalistic and utilitarian). Thus it is possible to view the psychiatrist as an 'agent of society', labelling non-conformists as officially *deviant*, and using the euphemism 'illness' to render the whole business more palatable to the apparently more humanitarian, civilized people of today.

The second aspect of the stigmatization phenomenon is that the evidence would suggest that society itself does not really believe in the concept of mental illness. As stated above, there is a tendency for psychiatric disorders to be regarded as permanent. In this respect, an admission to the local psychiatric hospital is considered to be almost equivalent socially to a period inside that other institution for nonconformists, the prison. Thus it is possible to view the whole situation as society colluding with the medical profession in order to expel deviants from our society in as humane a way as possible.

Even if one does not go so far as to view psychiatry as a

58

sophisticated twentieth-century version of the witch-burning game, one should at least be aware that it is by no means so clinical and impartial as it might appear at first sight.

## Summary and conclusions

Thus the medical model has, in effect, done comparatively little to increase our knowledge of disturbances of psychological functioning. In fact it could be argued that the illness analogy has actually obstructed original thinking in this highly complex area. The analogy itself is a weak one, in that medicine and psychiatry have very different notions as to the nature of health and illness. The most important discrepancy between the two is that whereas medicine is, by and large, an impartial discipline, psychiatry seems inevitably bound up with value systems. This effectively renders the psychiatrist more of a social judge than a detached clinician.

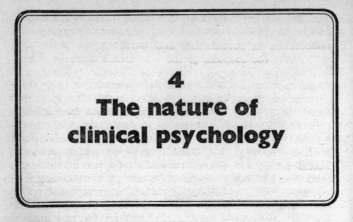

# 4
# The nature of clinical psychology

*A brief history*

The term 'clinical psychology' was first used by Witmer in 1896 to refer to assessment procedures which were carried out with retarded and physically-handicapped children. The establishment of the Vineland Institute for the investigation of mental retardation in 1906 and the Chicago Child Guidance Clinic in 1909 reflect the preoccupations with handicapped children of the pioneering psychologists in the clinical field. Although their interests later expanded to incorporate a whole variety of disorders, it is interesting to note that assessment was generally accepted to be the primary function of the applied psychologist throughout the first half of this century. A statement issued in 1935 by the clinical section of the American Psychological Association summarized the position as follows:

> Clinical Psychology aims to define the behaviour capacities and behaviour characteristics of an individual through methods of measurement, analysis and observation, and on the basis of an integration of these findings with data received from physical examinations and social histories, gives suggestions and recommendations for the proper adjustment of the individual.

In other words, the psychologist is portrayed as working alongside the social worker and medical doctor in an endeavour to produce the most appropriate treatment programme for the individual. More will be said about this so-called 'psychiatric team' at a later stage.

In the United Kingdom, the demand for psychological services in mental hospitals was generated following the collaboration of psychiatrists and psychologists which took place under the auspices of the War Office Selection Board (WOSB). Psychologists, with their scientific training, had proved themselves capable of devising assessment procedures of various sorts to assist in the selection of officers for the armed forces. On the basis of this, psychiatrists reasoned that it should prove possible to create similar tests in order to help psychiatrists classify their patients correctly. Thus clinical psychologists were appointed initially to devise objective clinical assessment procedures and subsequently to apply them when the psychiatrist encountered differential diagnosis problems. Following this, the Maudsley Hospital, the Crichton Royal Hospital and the Tavistock Clinic began offering training courses in clinical psychology, and the new applied discipline had finally arrived.

Even in these early days, however, there was little agreement between clinical psychologists as to the nature of the material they were to study, or as to the procedures they should adopt in order to do so. The Maudsley psychologists regarded themselves as experimental psychologists in abnormal psychology. In other words they perceived clinical psychology to be that form of academic psychology which uses psychiatric patients, as opposed to rats, as its subject matter. The Tavistock psychologists, on the other hand, claimed very little allegiance to general psychology and identified themselves far more with the non-experimental subject matter and methods of psychoanalytic theory. The result, inevitably, was friction between the two schools of thought and the rift between them is present even today.

The differences in theoretical orientation manifest themselves in the types of clinical work in which the two groups are involved. So far as assessment is concerned, those of a psychoanalytic persuasion generally employ projective techniques (see D3 and later) which, by their ambiguous nature, enable the skilled clinician to obtain material indicative of the unconscious conflicts which are presumed to underly the symptoms. Experimentally oriented psychologists, on the other hand, reject the notion of a dynamic unconscious and consequently feel little sympathy for such an approach to psychological assessment. Furthermore they are quick to point out the various research projects which have shown these tests to be unreliable and invalid. In view of the fact that they are by no means objective instruments, these psychologists do not regard them as tests in any meaningful sense, and consequently treat them with the disdain they normally reserve for such concepts as clinical intuition. In contrast, experimentalists, while hopefully awaiting the arrival of objective behavioural assessment procedures, make use of self-report inventories. These techniques require the individual to answer 'Yes', 'No', or (in some cases) 'Cannot say' to such questions as 'Do you often feel unhappy for no apparent reason?' However the fact that numerical scores can be derived from standardized questionnaires does little to disguise the fact that they constitute, in essence, controlled introspection. In other words their scientific responsibility is more apparent than real. Psychoanalytically-oriented psychologists are more concerned to criticize them on the grounds of superficiality and insensitivity.

From the therapeutic viewpoint, the experimentalists are highly critical of the psychoanalytic therapies on the grounds that the efficacy of these approaches has never been unequivocally demonstrated. Instead they engage in behaviour therapy (see p. 109) which, apparently, is based on experimentally derived principles, and which research has shown to be very effective with certain types of patients. Those who practise psychoanalytic therapies criticize the behavioural approach on the grounds that it constitutes a very superficial form of intervention and claim that, despite symptomatic improvement, the individual is left with his underlying problems. With such distinctive views as to the nature of man, it is hardly surprising that most people regard an eventual rapprochement between these two poles, in terms of actual clinical work, to be a pretty forlorn hope.

At the present time, clinical psychology seems to be spreading itself very thinly over a wide area and as new skills develop in each segment, so the disparity of interests between the various practitioners becomes more and more apparent. Apart from the obvious child/adult division there are research/applied, psychoanalytic/behaviourist, and assessment/treatment conflicts which do little for the unity of the discipline. Despite the youth of clinical psychology, many of the differences of opinion are at such a fundamental level as to suggest that any attempt to define the role of the clinical psychologist is doomed to failure at the outset. As Desai (1967) pointed out some years ago:

The question 'What is Clinical Psychology?' in terms of a body of knowledge and skills will be answered according to what particular school or schools of psychological thought one accepts. Indeed it would be difficult to say whether Clinical Psychology is a science, an attempt at a science or also something else. (p. 38)

The picture is certainly no clearer today.

*The functions of the clinical psychologist*
The lack of agreement between clinical psychologists as to the sort of services they should be providing can be both a drawback and a blessing in disguise. The disadvantage of this state of affairs is that the newly-appointed psychologist might find himself expected to contribute in particular ways which are discrepant from his own role expectations. On the other hand, the clinical psychologist can be seen to be in an almost unique position in the hospital setting in that, because of the ambiguous nature of the discipline, he can very often stipulate his own job description. Thus the lack of a clear-cut list of functions can work both for and against clinical psychologists.

Although each individual psychologist carves out a unique role for himself in the context of his particular institution, it is generally accepted (e.g. Desai, 1967) that there are four major services which the clinical psychologist can offer: assessment, treatment, teaching and research.

Since psychological treatments are examined in Part Two, the research methodology is consistent with that described elsewhere (see A1), and the teaching is fairly self-evident, the main emphasis here will be on assessment. This should certainly not be taken to imply that assessment is regarded as the most important of the four functions. The main reason for devoting so much to this aspect of the psychologist's work is that the whole issue of testing has become such a controversial one in psychology, and it is therefore important that the various points of view be considered in some detail.

*Assessment*
Testing has, until recently, been seen by both psychologists and psychiatrists to be the primary function of the clinical psychologist. With his training in methods of scientific inquiry, he is considered to be the best equipped person to devise and administer assessment instruments. These tests can be used to provide psychiatric diagnoses or to indicate the most appropriate course of action for the individual.

Although it might be expected that these two uses are synonymous, the fact that a diagnostic label, as a rule, provides little guidance as to how the individual should be treated makes it important to maintain this distinction.

*Tests as diagnostic labelling devices.* As was shown in Chapter two, the agreement between psychiatrists regarding specific diagnosis is not very high. The signs and symptoms are so ill-defined that it is difficult to allocate a person confidently to a particular group. Consequently the psychiatrist has to fall back on his 'clinical intuition' much of the time in order to fill up the space reserved for 'diagnosis' in the case notes. It was because of widespread dissatisfaction within the psychiatric profession at the unscientific nature of the assessment procedure that there was felt to be a need for the 'hard' data which psychometricians could supposedly provide. Thus the early clinical psychologists found themselves cast in the role of laboratory technicians, and had their functions limited to the administration of the psychological equivalent of blood tests.

By agreeing to play this part, clinical psychologists became easily assimilated into that central structure of medically-oriented psychiatry, 'the psychiatric team'. This somewhat ill-named committee generally comprises the following personnel:

1. *The psychiatrist* who, as head of the team, collects information from the others, makes the official diagnosis, and decides on the course of therapy.
2. *The psychiatric social worker* who provides details about the home situation along with any information gleaned from relatives and friends of the patient.
3. *The clinical psychologist* who administers batteries of tests in those cases where there is some query regarding the diagnosis and, in addition, provides descriptive material regarding intelligence and personality.
4. *The occupational therapist* who reports on the patient's performance in the recreational and work situations in the hospital.
5. *The psychiatric nurse* who provides information regarding the patient's general behaviour on the ward, and his relationships with other patients and the nursing staff.

In this archaic work group, the psychiatrist may find himself unable to formulate a diagnosis where a particular patient is concerned. For instance, the patient may be somewhat

64

elderly and have symptoms which are in keeping with a depressive picture. The question of whether the patient is clinically depressed and/or intellectually deteriorating is a difficult one to answer merely by interviewing him or watching his behaviour on the ward. In such a case, the psychologist may be asked to administer tests which have been devised specifically to distinguish between the two types of disorder. The psychologist then submits a report on the basis of the test results and the psychiatrist combines this information with information elicited from other members of the team in order to reach a diagnosis.

Before considering briefly some of the assessment procedures currently employed by clinical psychologists, it is important to be clear as to the precise nature of a psychological test (see E2). Kleinmuntz (1974) defines it as 'a standardized instrument or systematic procedure designed to obtain an objective measure of a sample of behaviour' (p. 69). Some of the important points in this definition require elaboration. By 'standardized' it is meant that the test should be of such a nature that it is presented in an identical fashion to all subjects. An 'objective measure' is a score which is arrived at by adding up certain clearly specified response characteristics in a manner which precludes any bias from the assessor. The 'sample of behaviour' implies the notion of representativeness. Clearly it is impossible to record everything a person says, thinks and feels in his many different life situations. Thus samples must be taken and some generalizations made from the hopefully representative data which is collected. The psychological tests which follow vary quite considerably in the extent to which they meet these various requirements.

The list of personality, intellectual, cognitive, perceptual, learning and memory tests, which have been devised by clinical psychologists for diagnostic purposes, is far too long to be considered here in full. Consequently, with the exception of personality, just one example of each type is considered briefly. In the case of personality, two illustrations are provided on account of the very different approaches adopted by those who use projective techniques and those who favour questionnaires.

*Personality tests*

(a) *Projective techniques*. The Rorschach ink-blot test consists of ten bilaterally symmetrical ink-blots, five of which are composed of differing shades of grey, two are made up of greys and colours, and three are completely coloured. The cards are presented one at a time to the subject who is instructed to report what he sees, what he is reminded of by the blot, and what the design means to him.

Although there are many scoring systems, the most formal ones take account of the *location* (i.e. part of the blot used for his response), *content* (e.g. human figures, anatomical diagrams) and *determinants* (e.g. form, colour) of the response. It is conjectured by some proponents of the Rorschach test (e.g. Alcock, 1963) that certain of these features are associated with particular types of disorder. For example, obsessive-compulsives apparently have a high percentage of responses which are based mainly on form, and tend to make more use of relatively small areas of the blot than do other groups. Patients with organic brain damage are supposed to make fewer responses than others, spend at least one minute over each response, make no more than one response involving movement, and repeat the same objects over again.

Despite its widespread use, the Rorschach has certainly not been without its critics. Baughman (1951) has demonstrated convincingly that the number and type of responses elicited from the subject are strongly influenced by the characteristics of the person who is administering the test. In other words the procedure does not meet the standardization requirements described above. Other critics have shown that there is poor agreement between diagnosis based on this test and diagnosis based on psychiatric interview. Furthermore, the Rorschach has been shown to be a poor predictor so far as response to therapy is concerned. For a summary of these and other criticisms of this technique, the reader is referred to the four excellent review articles which appeared in the *Fifth Mental Measurements Yearbook* (Buros, 1959).

Thus, although it may have its uses as an instrument for uncovering clinical material relevant to psychotherapy (see p. 86), the Rorschach falls far short of the requirements necessary for a diagnostic test.

(b) *Self-report inventories*. Many of the existing personality questionnaires have also been used for diagnostic purposes. The basic assumption made by their constructors is that pathological states are quantitatively, as opposed to qualitatively, different from states which are considered to be normal. This is by no means a universally accepted assumption and many workers (e.g. Foulds, 1961) maintain that there is a clear distinction between personality traits and diagnostic symptoms.

One of the best known examples of this type of test is Minnesota Multiphasic Personality Inventory (MMPI) (Hathaway and McKinley, 1951). It consists of 550 affirmative statements, printed on separate cards, which the subject is asked to classify into three categories: True, False and Cannot Say. The statements cover such areas as health, political attitudes, motor disturbances and manifestations of psychopathological behaviour.

When first published, the MMPI provided scores on nine clinical scales, representing the various types of psychiatric disorders. These are: hypochondriasis, depression, hysteria, psychopathic deviate, masculinity-femininity, paranoia, psychasthenia (obsolete term meaning neurotic), schizophrenia and hypomania. Since then a tenth scale, social introversion, has been added. In addition the MMPI has four 'check scales', called the question, lie, validity and correction scores, which attempt to ensure that the clinical scores are a true reflection of the characteristics of the individual. An atlas of coded profiles, together with 968 short case histories, has been produced by Hathaway and Meehl (1951) to help the clinician formulate diagnoses from test results.

Many of the problems associated with this instrument are directly due to the fact that it was initially validated against the Kraepelinian diagnostic categories. Recent factor analytic studies (e.g. Adams, 1964), however, would suggest that there are insufficient grounds for grouping the various items under their traditional headings. The test has also been criticized on the grounds of poor test/retest reliability, so far as some of the scales are concerned. The size and representativeness of the normative sample, which has provided the data from which the pre-profile standard scores are derived, has been described as inadequate (Anastasi, 1968). Another reason for disenchantment with this technique concerns the fact that it comprises a conglomeration of items relating to personality traits and signs and symptoms of psychopathology. Thus the interpreter has to operate simultaneously as a personality assessor and a diagnostician.

*Intelligence tests*
In addition to its major use as a measure of intellectual functioning, the Wechsler Adult Intelligence Scale (WAIS) (Wechsler, 1955) has also been employed as a diagnostic instrument. The test consists of eleven sub-tests, six of which are verbal (i.e. based on words) and five of which are per-

formance (i.e. of a perceptual/motor kind). One crude sign of psychopathology is considered to be the *scatter*, or extent of variation, among the sub-test scores. Wechsler (1958) provides some data obtained from schizophrenic and normal groups to support his hypothesis that a wide range of scores is indicative of psychiatric disturbances. However, many others (e.g. Patterson, 1953) argue that the range of scores is worthless for diagnostic purposes because of the fact that large discrepancies can be accounted for in terms of educational, occupational and cultural factors.

Many attempts have been made to link up patterns of subtest distribution with specific disorders. Some of these 'systems' of analysis, with their credibility seemingly based almost entirely on the clinical intuition of their constructors (e.g. Schafer, 1948), seem somewhat reminiscent of the less structured type of Rorschach interpretation. Wechsler's own approach to the question of the clinical interpretation of subtest score patterns is more empirically based. He has described patterns for organic brain disorders, schizophrenia, anxiety states, juvenile delinquency and mental deficiency on the basis of his research with such groups (Wechsler, 1958).

As a diagnostic test, the WAIS has been attacked (e.g. Anastasi, 1968) on the grounds that although it may be possible to find statistical trends between groups, the test does not permit the psychologist to classify any one patient with any degree of confidence. A second limitation concerns the fact that the reliabilities of the sub-tests are not high enough to allow the clinician to make an unequivocal interpretation (McNemar, 1957). Finally, the fact that other workers have obtained results with pathological groups which are not in keeping with Wechsler's findings (e.g. Rabin and Guertin, 1951) has led to the gradual abandonment of the WAIS as a diagnostic tool. Nevertheless it is still considered to be valuable clinically in throwing up hypotheses which can be tested by more specialized instruments.

*Cognitive tests*

The Grid Test of Schizophrenic Thought Disorder (Bannister and Fransella, 1967) is a diagnostic test derived from Kelly's Personal Construct Theory (see Ch. 8). It consists of eight head and shoulder photographs, four of men and four of women. The subject is provided with the first construct, 'kind', and is asked to say which of the people in the photographs is the kindest, who is the next kindest, and so on until he has rank ordered all eight photographs on this concept. He is then asked to do the same thing with the other five constructs which are 'stupid', 'selfish', 'sincere', 'mean' and 'honest'. The whole test is then repeated. The two scores which emerge from this are *intensity* (I) (i.e. the extent to which the various constructs intercorrelate) and *consistency* (C) (i.e. the degree of concordance between the two sets of results).

In the preliminary validation study, it was demonstrated that the I/C scores could distinguish thought-disordered schizophrenics from non-thought-disordered schizophrenics, depressives, neurotics, organics and normals. Subsequent research, however, has failed to support the strong claims made for it by its authors. In a study by Foulds *et al.* (1967), only 50 per cent of thought-disordered schizophrenics obtained scores within the required range. Poole's study (1968) found no significant relationship between clinical assessment of thought disorder and scores on this test.

It could of course be argued that the relatively low correlation between the clinical and psychometric assessments of thought disorder really reflect the poor standard of psychiatric judgement rather than the invalidity of this test. However the fact that the test itself was originally validated against clinical impressions makes it difficult to draw a firm conclusion either way.

## Perceptual tests

One of the earliest tests to be used in clinical practice was the Bender Visual Motor Gestalt Test (Bender, 1938), or Bender-Gestalt Test as it is now known. In this test, nine simple diagrams are presented individually on cards to the subject, with the instructions that he is to copy what he sees. The particular designs used in this test were constructed to illustrate certain principles of Gestalt psychology (see A4) and, in fact, the test results were originally analysed, albeit somewhat unsystematically, according to Gestaltist principles.

The first real standardization of this test was undertaken by Pascal and Suttell (1951), who produced a relatively objective scoring key on the basis of their findings regarding the errors which differentiated normals from abnormals. They then carried out a cross-validation study of this new key with normals, neurotics and psychotics and successfully distinguished between these groups. Other workers have been more interested in observing signs which are characteristic of particular types of disorder. Gobetz (1953), for instance, produced a list of response features which he claimed distinguished neurotics from normals.

The main problem with tests such as this is that because they have been shown to discriminate significantly between various diagnostic groups, it does not follow that a great deal of reliance can be placed on their findings regarding the individual patient. And, after all, it is this which the clinician is most interested in.

## Learning/memory tests

The Walton-Black Modified New Word Learning Test (Walton and Black, 1957) was devised as a differential test for brain damage. The procedure is as follows. A list of words, taken from the vocabulary scales of some intelligence tests, are read to the patient one at a time in progressive order of difficulty, and he is asked to provide a definition of each. This part of the procedure is terminated when he fails to provide the meanings of ten consecutive words. The ten words are then read out with their definitions. After this, the words are presented on their own once again and the subject is asked to say what each one means. The whole procedure is repeated, with variations in the supplied definitions, until the subject is able to give six correct responses on any one trial. The score is based on the number of trials the subject required in order to reach the criterion. In the original validation study, it was demonstrated that the test could distinguish organics from normals, neurotics, psychotics and mental defectives, although several in the latter group were wrongly classified as organic.

One problem with this test concerns the fact that many old people who suffer from dysphasia might be wrongly classified as intellectually deteriorating on a test which makes use of verbal material exclusively. A second problem is that the administration of this test is, of necessity, not completely standardized. Since different words are used with each subject, it is possible that some might receive longer and more complex definitions than others. Despite these limitations, the test has proved more useful clinically than many other tests of brain damage.

## Critical comment

One of the most disappointing aspects of abnormal psychology concerns the split which exists between theories of psychopathology and the tests which are employed in the clinic. On the one hand, clinicians in general have been concerned to find any tool which can help to solve differential diagnostic problems, regardless of whether it has emerged from a long line of research or from off the top of someone's head. 'If it works use it' seems to be the slogan. Researchers in abnormal psychology, on the other hand, have been more interested in testing out their hypotheses regarding particular disorders than in devising sensitive clinical instruments based on their theories.

Tolor and Schulberg (1963) are typical of those who believe that so far as assessment is concerned, empirical research on its own is rarely of much value. In their critique of the Bender-Gestalt test, they deplore the lack of 'theoretical underpinning' and the 'preponderance of low level conceptualization' involved in its construction. This ill-conceived instrument is very much in contrast to the Bannister-Fransella test which evolved directly from Bannister's theories concerning the genesis of schizophrenia (see Ch. 8). Although, as has already been shown, there are problems associated with this test, it deserves special mention because of the fact that it constitutes a clinical extension of a theory of psychopathology. It is essential in my view that clinical psychologists should base their tests on sound theoretical backgrounds where possible if any real advances in the understanding of abnormal psychology are to be made.

A second problem with psychology tests is the tendency for them to be viewed as valid clinical instruments just because it has been shown that they can differentiate between groups of disorders in the initial study. The clinical psychologist, however, is concerned with the individual case. With tests such as the Bender-Gestalt, where there is a great deal of overlap between groups, he is unable to make a definite decision in any but the most extreme cases. The Kendrick battery is one of the regrettably few tests which have been repeatedly modified in order to decrease the likelihood of misclassification. It is unfortunate that in the past so many test constructors have felt that their work is done because significant differences have been obtained between groups.

The third problem concerns the criteria against which the majority of tests have been validated. So far as organic disorders are concerned, the situation is fairly straightforward in that knowledge of the occurrence of severe head injury can be taken as providing fairly unequivocal evidence of brain pathology. However, so far as the other disorders are concerned, the standards against which the tests are measured are usually in the form of psychiatric ratings. But as Smail (1973) points out, 'Using diagnostic tests validated against psychiatric opinion to suggest to psychiatrists what their diagnostic opinion should be makes use of an indefensible logic and renders absurd a significant amount of the way many of us have to spend our time.' (p. 213)

It is, of course, assumed that by validating the test against psychiatric opinion where the cases are clear-cut, then in those situations where the psychiatrist is undecided as to the diagnosis, the test will provide the correct answer. But there is, unfortunately, no evidence to suggest that the test can do any better in equivocal cases than the psychiatrist. What makes the whole situation so ludicrous is that the psychiatrist will only refer a patient for assessment if he constitutes a differential diagnosis problem. Thus the test is never required for use with the sort of population it has been validated on.

The final criticism is just a reiteration of the arguments against the whole notion of diagnosis. Since there seems to be less and less evidence that the homogeneous, independent disease entities envisaged by Kraepelin actually exist, it would seem utterly pointless for psychologists to continue to attempt to carry out diagnostic assessment in order to support a seemingly erroneous conceptual system. Furthermore, even in those few cases where the psychologist finds someone who closely resembles 'the typical schizophrenic' in terms of response patterns, it is unlikely that this rare psychometric achievement will have much bearing on the treatment the patient receives. The last word on this issue belongs to Bannister (1969):

> In current practice, the origin of the psychological investiga-
> tion is usually a problem misformulated by a psychologically
> untrained psychiatrist and the results of the psychological
> investigation are fed back into the confused context of the
> operations of the same psychologically untrained psychiatrist.
> Thus there is a divorce between investigation, measurement
> and testing on the one hand, and intervention, modification
> and change on the other. This arbitrary division of thought by
> division of labour has rendered sterile much of the testing
> done by psychologists. It has given rise to the nightmare of
> 'meter reading' as the model for clinical psychology. (p. 300)

*Test as indicators to action.* There has been a recent trend in clinical psychology for assessment to be shunned altogether and dismissed as both a pointless and a degrading exercise.

In their attempts to dispel any lingering notions that they are in any way professionally inferior to psychiatrists, status-sensitive psychologists have tended to discontinue their psychometric function with its laboratory technician image. This is a regrettable turn of events, in my opinion, because psychological tests can provide objective information which cannot be collected by any other means. This information can then be used to help decide the therapeutic programme which is to be instigated for the individual patient. Thus although I hold the 'diagnosis please' referral in very low regard, it would seem to me quite appropriate to use standardized instruments to answer such questions as 'What approach should be taken with this individual?' Some of the broad areas where psychological tests have, I feel, something to offer are as follows:

*Psychotherapy.* Many of the major schools of psychotherapy have assessment procedures associated with them which are based on the same basic theoretical principles. Since they operate within a common conceptual framework, data from the testing situation in such cases can be fed directly into the therapy situation and vice versa. Thus, for instance, tests can be administered at the beginning of therapy to help elicit the objectives of therapy and the general approach to be taken. They can also be used at varying intervals throughout therapy to assess its efficacy, and to monitor any change in goals that might have taken place. Finally the tests can be used towards the end of therapy in order to demonstrate to both therapist and patient that the objectives have been reached and that termination should be being considered. The whole purpose of assessment is seen in a completely different light in those cases where the therapy and the test complement each other. Such procedures as projective tests, behavioural sampling and the repertory grid technique are used in this way. Details of the ways in which they operate alongside their associated therapies are provided at a later stage (see pp. 86, 115, 127).

*Remedial training/rehabilitation.* One particularly useful function of psychological tests is to describe the precise nature and extent of the abilities of the individual. This is particularly so in the field of child psychology. Thus, for instance, where the language or reading abilities of the child are retarded, psychological assessment can help to determine whether this involves a perceptual and/or motor dysfunction, whether it is a problem of general comprehension, or whether it is personality related. The test findings can therefore be used to devise the most appropriate treatment programmes for the individual case.

Psychological assessment has a similar part to play with patients who have received head injuries leading to impairment of mental functions. There would seem to be little point in administering diagnostic tests, in such cases, to determine whether he has 'brain damage' or not. A far more important question to ask, from the point of view of management, is 'What sorts of things does he find difficult to do?' With such a referral, the very nature of the care he receives from doctors, nurses, physiotherapists and occupational therapists can be determined by the answers which the test provides. Thus an intensive analysis of the patient's psychological functioning can yield much more information of a practical nature than just attempting to fit him into a diagnostic class.

*Vocational guidance.* It is my view that referrals for intelligence and personality assessment should be discouraged in those cases where the referral source has no clear idea as to why he is seeking such data and, what is more, how he is going to make use of it once it has been obtained. There is a regrettable tendency for many psychiatrists to ask for such tests to be carried out merely in order to satisfy their curiosity, to augment a presentation at a case conference, or because they have no idea what to do and are hoping that a solution will emerge with the accumulation of multi-source information. This seems to me to be a gross mis-use of the psychologist's skills.

There are, however, instances where decisions regarding the management of the individual could be influenced by such test results. One situation where it would seem perfectly reasonable to seek information about level of intellectual functioning and personality characteristics is where there is a hypothesis that the unsuitability of current employment is a major factor contributing to the patient's distress. Jobs which either over- or under-tax the person's abilities, or clash with his traits or interests, can cause, or at least exacerbate, psychological problems. Consequently detailed knowledge of the individual's characteristics can be extremely useful so far as specific recommendations regarding employment are concerned.

Thus far from being an irrelevant and debasing activity, assessment, when used in an appropriate manner, can provide clear-cut guidelines for the way in which the patient is treated by all who are connected with the case.

## Therapy

With psychologists becoming more and more disillusioned with assessment, it was hardly surprising that they should seek to expand their role as agents of behaviour change. Consequently dramatic advances in various psychological therapies have accompanied the decline of the psychological test. Due to sensitivity concerning the scientific nature of clinical psychology, a large proportion of the profession have sought training in behaviour modification (see Ch. 7), with its foundations apparently firmly embedded in academic psychology. Thus despite the fact that there has always been a hard core of psychologists who are committed to psychoanalytically-oriented psychotherapy, there has not been an equivalent rise in the number of its practitioners in recent years. Presumably one contributing factor here is that the untestability of many of the assumptions underlying this approach has failed to attract those who have graduated from the more experimentally-biased psychology courses. That this is not the only reason is borne out by the fact that many psychologists, particularly in the United States, have become very involved in the humanistic/existentialistic forms of therapy in recent years. These 'third force' psychologists are also, on the whole, sceptical as to the value of traditional scientific experimentation. Perhaps the real explanation as to why psychologists have become so involved in behaviour therapy on the one hand and in the unorthodox therapies on the other is that, since both approaches are relatively new, psychologists have a greater opportunity for developing their separate identity by adhering to them than if they were to swell the ranks of the medically-dominated psychoanalysts. This interpretation of the events is, of course, highly speculative.

Since the second section of this book is devoted to psychosocial models and the associated methods of effecting change, no attempt will be made to elaborate here on the types of therapy which psychologists have to offer. In this country, behaviour modification (see p. 109) and psychoanalytic psychotheraphy (see p. 91) are the most readily available psychological treatments, with personal construct therapy (see p.

127) and client-centred therapy (see p. 100) now gradually beginning to make some sort of impact.

*Teaching*
Clinical psychologists have a very important function to perform in instructing psychiatrists, social workers, occupational therapists and nurses in basic psychological principles. The training courses associated with each of these professions recognize the importance of a grounding in psychology and attempt to provide some coverage of the main topics. This is, however, rarely adequate and the psychologist finds himself devoting a lot of time in attempting to make this material pertinent to these groups in their particular work situations.

In addition, the psychologist often finds himself carrying out more specialized forms of teaching. The training and supervision of other members of staff in therapeutic techniques is one very important example. Instructing, say, occupational therapists as to how to make use of psychological test results when designing treatment programmes is another. Where ward management schemes are being implemented, it is absolutely essential that the nursing staff are well informed as to the overall purpose, as well as to the actual mechanics, of the whole operation.

Thus teaching should not be regarded as a routine chore by the clinical psychologist, but as an essential part of his work if he is to exert much influence on his colleagues and thereby fully develop his other roles.

*Research*
Psychologists are far better trained to conduct research projects than any of their professional colleagues. Both as undergraduates and as postgraduates they have been schooled in the intricacies of experimental design and statistical procedures, and have been involved in a wide range of psychological experiments. It is not surprising, therefore, that one of the functions of the clinical psychologist in the psychiatric setting is, not only to carry out his own research projects, but to encourage and assist others to carry out projects themselves.

Some of the main types of research projects in the field of abnormal psychology are as follows:

1 Carrying out animal experiments in order to set up hypotheses of psychiatric disorders (e.g. Seligman and Maier, 1967).

76

2 Testing out hypotheses regarding the precise nature of the psychological disturbance in the various psychiatric groups (e.g. Bannister, 1963).
3 Investigating the causes of psychological disturbances (e.g. Mednick, 1970).
4 Comparing the effectiveness of different forms of treatment (e.g. Paul, 1966).
5 Looking for signs which might enable one to predict the likelihood of a particular patient recovering (Vaillant, 1966).

One of the problems with the bulk of the research which clinical psychologists have carried out is that it is very much based on the disease concept notion in psychiatry. In other words, psychologists have been concerned to isolate the *aetiological* factors (causes), describe the *symptoms* more accurately, determine the *prognosis* (estimate the probability of eventual improvement), and compare *treatments*, just as medical scientists might approach a newly discovered physical illness. This is understandable in view of the fact that more elegant experimental designs can be employed if subjects can meaningfully be divided up into discrete categories. Thus, researchers in the field of abnormal psychology have a lot invested in the notion of mental illness and are unwilling to abandon it. However, if the individual rather than the disorder is to become the focal point of the applied discipline, then intensive single-subject research would seem to be far more appropriate than inter-group studies. As yet, few research-oriented clinical psychologists have followed their therapeutically-minded colleagues in this direction.


### The identity of clinical psychology

The developmental history of clinical psychology, as will have been gathered from the previous pages, could hardly be described as incident-free. Having spent its early years being fostered by an alien discipline, it has grown up in the knowledge that this parent figure of psychiatry has itself been misguided and has, through the years, been unwittingly stunting the growth of its charge. As a result, clinical psychology has emerged as a somewhat sickly adolescent with little idea as to what it is, or how it fits in with those around it. This 'identity crisis' would seem to centre round what Bannister (1969) calls the 'science' issue and the 'medical' issue.

The *science issue* concerns the fact that psychologists are trained to perceive themselves as behavioural scientists. In other words they are taught to mistrust subjective impressions, unsupported assumptions and uncontrolled observations. The 'truth' is considered to be something which can only be arrived at through controlled experimentation and the diligent accumulation of objective data. One can therefore appreciate the dilemma in which the clinical psychologist, with such a background, finds himself: he is faced with largely impotent psychometric devices, on the one hand, and less standardized but more clinically relevant tests on the other. Further, he uses therapeutic techniques which, despite the academic respectability of their underlying principles, still incorporate many variables which are outside the control of the practitioner. The question he asks himself is whether he can fulfil the functions of the clinical psychologist and still regard himself as a behavioural scientist. Bannister (1969) however expresses little patience with those who refuse to engage in psychotherapy because of its reputedly unscientific nature: 'The obvious flaw in this argument is that it assumes that where scientific endeavour is difficult, we cease to be scientists; instead of accepting that we simply become scientists who are working harder than usual' (p. 299).

The *medical issue* refers to the fact that many clinical psychologists are unwilling to conduct therapy because, in the first place, they consider treatment to be the province of the medically trained; and, secondly, because of the dreaded medical-model connotations surrounding it, feel that they would be betraying their psychological heritage. These points will be considered separately.

The question of who should carry out therapy is one which has caused more friction between psychology and psychiatry than any other. On the one hand, it would appear that many psychiatrists feel threatened by the advances which psychologists have made in the therapeutic field, and seek to discourage this trend. Slater and Roth (1969), for instance, take a very conservative position on this matter:

One method of closing the gap between psychology and psychiatry is, however, to be regarded with some reserve, namely the tendency shown for the psychologist, for example, in the application of learning theory in therapy, to take over the functions of a doctor and to engage in individual treatment. Some psychologists have shown unusual ability in this field, and it would be a pity if they were discouraged. However, the selection of cases for such treatment should always be made by the doctor and psychiatrist. (p. 10)

Many frustrated psychologists, on the other hand, see the situation somewhat differently: 'Today it may well be true that a newly fledged basic grade psychologist is much better informed about, and able to practise *psychological* treatment of, many of the major forms of functional "mental illness" than is (the) average consultant...' (Smail, 1973, p. 213). Clearly there are no small differences of opinion on this issue.

From a purely technical viewpoint, the current situation in the United Kingdom (at present under review) is that a medically-qualified person must take responsibility for any therapy which is carried out. Thus a psychologist cannot carry out a treatment programme unless a doctor has agreed to provide medical cover. In my own experience, this has never been a problem, in that I have always felt free to carry out any type of therapy I so desired. However it is, I understand, not unknown for psychiatrists to interfere with the psychologist's work or overrule his decisions. In the final analysis, the most important factors concerning the working relationship between the psychologist and the psychiatrist are the personalities involved. This is obviously an unsatisfactory situation and one hopefully to be remedied in the near future. In the meantime one can sympathize with those clinical psychologists who avoid friction by refusing to engage in therapy.

Feelings of antipathy for the medical model is not such a strong case for not carrying out behaviour change. It is quite feasible to view oneself as utilizing an educational model where terms such as 'training' and 'objectives' replace 'treatment' and 'cure' (see E3). This is not purely a matter of semantics since the way in which the problem and intervention are conceptualized will affect both the psychologist's and client's approach to the task.

Thus clinical psychologists, at this stage, are still very much concerned with establishing their professional identity. They tend to be viewed as 'soft' and 'unscientific' by academic psychologists and as 'unqualified to treat' by many psychiatrists. The answer to the first point is that they are using the scientific approach, in the broad sense of setting up and testing hypotheses and controlling variables, but are simply working with more complex and less tangible problems. The answer to the second is that it is anticipated that in the near future the recognition of psychologists as bona fide therapists will change from mere convention to statute.

## Summary and conclusions

The history of psychology within psychiatry has been a very stormy one, and is particularly remarkable for the strife which has taken place between psychology and psychiatry. Certainly the functions of psychologists have changed over the years. Psychological tests are now considered to be of little value as mere diagnostic instruments and to be used more in order to make decisions regarding the treatment programme for the individual. Clinical psychologists are now far more involved in carrying out therapy than they were, particularly of a behavioural kind. In addition, teaching and research are still considered to be important parts of the services which the psychologist has to offer in the psychiatric setting. With alterations in the importance of the four functions, it is hardly surprising that clinical psychology is currently experiencing problems in establishing its identity. There are however encouraging signs that these changes of emphasis are being recognized by outside bodies. It is anticipated that statutory adjustments will take place in the near future to reduce the discrepancy between what psychologists want to do and what they are allowed to do. This should go a long way towards clarifying the nature and identity of the discipline.

# Part Two
# Psychosocial approaches to psychiatric disorders

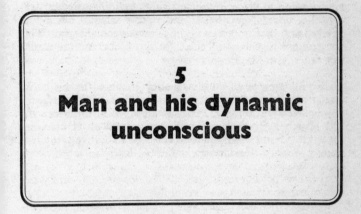

# 5
# Man and his dynamic unconscious

The work of Sigmund Freud (see C1, D3) has undoubtedly had more impact on psychology, philosophy, medicine and the arts than that of any other writer on psychological matters. There are indeed few aspects of our culture which have not been influenced, directly or indirectly, by the ideas of the founder of psychoanalysis. Despite his fame, however, his stature in the academic and clinical fields is due less to the fact that he succeeded in devising a comprehensive theory of personality with its associated therapeutic techniques, than to the fact that he introduced an important new concept into psychology – the dynamic unconscious. Freud's innovative proposal that the mind can be compared to an iceberg, with the great bulk of it below the surface, is very much the cornerstone of this theory and of those of most of the analysts who came after him. In his view the unconscious mind, which by definition is inaccessible by direct means, provides the psychic energy, or 'dynamism', which causes the individual to function. Such a controversial idea has, not unnaturally, provoked a lot of antagonism from scientists with both a psychological and medical background. However, despite intense criticism over the years from these sources, the concept of the unconscious has proved remarkably resilient and, although its precise nature and functions have been the cause of much dispute between the various psychodynamic schools, it has survived up to the present day.

Many of his other hypotheses have not stood the test of time so well; indeed, few contemporary psychotherapists would admit to being Freudians without adding some qualification or other. Nevertheless, his psychoanalytical model has been chosen here to represent the psychodynamic approach on the grounds that it is still the most systematic and influential one of its type.

*General approach.* Of all the theories presented in this book, Freud's is the most difficult to locate in terms of the medical/psychological dichotomy. Freud was trained in medicine and this reveals itself in the clinical flavour of much of his writings. The notion that symptoms must be indicative of underlying pathology, for instance, adheres closely to the concept of disease. Furthermore, evaluative concepts such as *normal* personality development and sexual *perversions* are very much in keeping with the mental illness approach.

On the other hand, he tended to focus more on the individual than on disease entities, which is not a practice normally associated with medically-oriented thinkers. The fact that he was often referred to as a 'teacher' rather than a 'therapist' might suggest that he was really employing an educational model. However the main reason for regarding his theory as a psychosocial one is that he postulated that faulty interpersonal relationships, particularly familial ones, had a part to play in the genesis of psychological disturbances.

Freud's basic position can be summarized as follows. He saw man as being dominated by biological instincts, which are both constructive and destructive in nature, as well as by other unconscious desires of various sorts. Because these primitive motives are constantly clashing with the socialized aspects of the personality, the individual is portrayed as going through life attempting to deal with such intrapsychic conflicts. In his attempts to defend against the anxiety produced by such disharmony, he tends to engage in irrational and maladaptive behaviour. Thus psychiatric symptoms are seen as mere superficial representations of deep-seated unresolved conflicts. The well-adjusted person is considered to be the individual who reaches a compromise position whereby he is achieving maximal instinctual gratification while experiencing minimal guilt.

Thus the psychoanalytic approach takes a very deterministic and negativistic view of human nature, with little room for such humanistic notions as 'personal growth' and 'free will'. It is equally pessimistic where group behaviour is concerned in that, for example, war is viewed as an inevitable product of man's destructive instincts.

*Theoretical rationale.* Freud's basic proposition is that all psychic energy stems from instincts which are persistently expressing themselves and are represented mentally as emotionally charged ideas (cathexis). One of the fundamental drives, the 'life' instinct (Eros) manifests itself through an energy source, primarily of a sexual nature, termed the *libido*. During the first year of life, libidinal energy becomes centred around the mouth and lips (oral stage) and the child at this time derives sensual pleasure from sucking and, eventually, biting. After this, the libido transfers itself partially to the anal region of the body and the child now derives pleasure from the retention and expulsion of faeces (anal stage). In these early stages the child's interests are largely concentrated on himself (narcissism) and relationships with other people are confined to parts of their bodies, such as the nipple. At about the age of three, the penis or clitoris becomes the main erogenous zone and the child tends to engage in masturbation at this time (phallic stage). Once this stage has been reached, object relationships tend to be extended to the whole person.

One of the most important conflicts in his whole developmental history takes place as the child is passing through this particular phase. Freud believed that each young boy has symbolically to undergo the experience of the Greek mythological character, Oedipus, who unwittingly killed his father and married his mother. Thus between the ages of three and five, the boy is thought to develop incestuous longings for his mother and simultaneously to view his father as a rival for his mother's affections. However he is frightened by the thought of competing with the authority figure in the family and feels that his father may become angry and punish him by cutting off his penis (castration anxiety). The name for this dilemma is the *Oedipus complex*. As a result of this anxiety, he is forced to repress his erotic feelings for his mother and identify with his father. Resolution of the conflict in this way is thought to be essential if the individual is to be able to engage in heterosexual relationships when he reaches maturity.

Freud believed that each girl at this time went through a reciprocal conflict (the *Electra complex*), although his descriptions of this phenomenon are far less lucid. Apparently she experiences a strong desire to renounce her femininity and become a male (penis envy). At the same time she blames her mother for her lack of a phallus, and experiences sensual desires regarding her father. Again the solution is for her to repress her inappropriate feelings towards both parents and to resolve the whole situation by identifying with her mother.

The phallic stage is followed by the latency stage, where sexual motivation recedes in importance as the child becomes preoccupied with the development of skills. After puberty, the dramatic changes in glandular activities lead to increased libido, and, provided the Oedipal or Electra complex has been resolved adequately, the adolescent becomes sexually interested in extra-familial members of the opposite sex (genital stage).

Normal sexual development is hampered when the *libido* becomes fixated at one of the early erogenous zones. Generally this is thought to occur because of too much or too little gratification at the stage associated with that particular part of the body. As well as preventing the individual from fully maturing sexually, fixation also provides the individual with an immature state to *regress* to when frustrated or faced with stress. This can be shown in different ways. Thus Freud claimed that sexual perversions are examples of positive expressions of libidinal fixation, whereas negative expressions take the form of neurotic disorders.

Superimposed on his theory of psychosexual development, is his portrayal of the composition of the mind. Freud conceived of the psyche as comprising three separate subsystems and, although he regarded them as being somewhat arbitrary, he retained this conceptual schema throughout his writings. The three subdivisions are as follows:

The *id* is presumed to be the primitive instinctive portion of the mind. As well as Eros (see above), it includes the 'death' instinct (Thanatos), which is considered to be the self-destructive force in the personality. The id operates according to the *pleasure principle*, in that it is concerned purely with the gratification of basic needs. It is entirely selfish and makes no allowances for reality or moral considerations. In itself it is unable to meet these demands, although it can generate wish-fulfilling fantasies and images related to these needs.

As the child gradually learns to differentiate between himself and his world, so the *ego* develops and serves to mediate between the demands of the id and the restrictions imposed by external reality. The ego is concerned to meet the demands of the id but in such a way as not to jeopardize the well-being of the individual. Because reason and judgement are utilized in the procedure of adaptation, the ego is said to operate according to the *reality principle*.

The third subsystem, the *superego*, is that portion of the personality which has taken over the restrictive and prohibitive functions of the parents. This corresponds to the lay term 'conscience'. As it develops, the superego often comes into direct conflict with the primitive desires of the id, and consequently strives to compel the ego to inhibit those activities which it considers to be 'wrong'. The ability of the ego to handle such conflicts is considered to be a key factor in determining the degree of adjustment of the individual.

In classical Freudian theory, psychoneurotic disturbances are thought to be due primarily to repression of experiences, usually of a sexual or aggressive nature and particularly those involving parents. The mechanism of repression is employed to remove the fear of punishment or withdrawal of love by the parents, which has been internalized by the superego. Since the disturbing material is never made available to the ego, the conflicts are never resolved and a certain degree of reality distortion has, of necessity, to take place from the period of trauma onwards. Another result of the whole process is that the use of repression and other defence mechanisms (ways of defending the ego) deprive the individual of large amounts of energy which should be being utilized as he passes through subsequent stages of development. Thus, due to the excessive use of defence mechanisms, he misses out on some vital experiences and finds himself unable to cope with demands that are made on him in adulthood.

*Assessment.* Since the psychoanalytic approach regards behavioural disturbances as mere signs of underlying and unresolved conflicts, it follows that the associated assessment techniques should be more concerned with eliciting the nature of the presumed psychopathology than with describing and measuring the symptoms. The problem here is that the deep-seated source of tension is not directly accessible and consequently any method of inquiry has somehow to circumvent the ever-watchful superego. Psychologists, with a psycho-analytical background, claim that projective techniques provide one means whereby this can be achieved.

All projective techniques are based on the assumption that when an individual is asked to impose meaning or order on an ambiguous stimulus, his attempts to do so will, unknown to him, reveal his secret feelings and desires. The tests themselves make use of such diverse overt tasks as story construction (e.g. Thematic Apperception Test), association to stimuli (e.g. Rorschach Ink-blot Test), sentence completion, artistic creation (e.g. Draw-a-Person Test), stimulus evaluation (e.g. Szondi Test) and self-expression (e.g. Psychodrama). The factor which all these tests have in common is that they make use of relatively unstructured and ambiguous material which requires the individual to make his own sense out of them.

Unfortunately, from the scientific point of view, the un-standardized nature of these tests, with the possible exception of sentence completion devices, requires each individual psychologist to make his own sense out of the responses of his patients. Thus it is possible to regard them as much projective tests for psychologists as for patients! Hence it is extremely difficult to evaluate the clinical usefulness of such tests. Anastasi (1968) summarizes the position by stating that the value of these techniques 'is not proportional to the skill of the clinician and hence cannot be assessed independently of the individual clinician using them' (p. 518).

Finally it should be emphasized that, although these tests can be employed diagnostically (see p. 66), they are not normally used in such a mechanistic fashion. The main value of these instruments would seem to be as material-eliciting devices for use in psychotherapy with the individual patient. Since both treatment and assessment are based on the same theoretical principles, it would appear that these techniques might have an important role to play in this specific context. Their use in other ways is more open to question.

*Methods of effecting change.* The ultimate aim of therapy is to restore to consciousness the material which has been repressed and which is required for personality growth. In classical psychoanalysis, the relationship which the patient establishes with the therapist helps to strengthen the ego so that it will be able to cope with the anxiety caused by the return to awareness of the 'forgotten' feelings and events. In order that the patient should focus on the derivatives of the repressed material, the form of treatment is organized so as to keep references to current reality situations to a bare minimum. This is achieved by the technique of 'free association', the recumbent position of the patient on the couch, the non-obtrusiveness of the therapist, and the emphasis on dreams and fantasies.

The whole basis of psychoanalysis centres round the phenomenon of *transference*. Although, in the early years, Freud felt that the irrational feelings that patients tended to have for their therapists constituted an obstacle to therapy, he eventually came to realize that transference might play 'a decisive part in bringing conviction not only to the patient but also to the physician' (Freud, 1909). The whole procedure can in fact be regarded as a sophisticated form of projective technique. Throughout therapy, the psychoanalyst refrains from showing emotions; he never evaluates attitudes expressed by the patient, and under no circumstances reveals personal information regarding himself. By maintaining his anonymity and thereby creating an ambiguous stimulus of himself, the therapist becomes the object onto which the patient's repressed feelings are projected.

The precise nature of transference has caused much dissension within psychoanalytic circles over the years. According to Sandler *et al.* (1970), Freud viewed transference as 'the displacement of libido from the memory of the original object to the person of the analyst, who became the new object of the patient's sexual wishes, the patient being unaware of this process of displacement from the past' (p. 669). Later writers, however, have proposed that transference should not be regarded as a phenomenon exclusive to the psychoanalytic situation but instead as a common psychological occurrence. Greenson (1965), for instance, states that 'for a reaction to be considered transference it must have two characteristics: it must be a repetition of the past and it must be inappropriate to the present' (p. 156). Many psychoanalysts, however, feel that such a broad definition could lead to imprecise thinking, and thus advocate that transference should only be used to refer to feelings which were not present at the beginning of therapy and which have emerged as a result of it.

According to Freud (1920), sometimes manifestations of transference become so intense that the patient re-enacts with the therapist conflict situations and traumatic experiences which have long been repressed. These reproductions are always associated with infantile sexuality and are carried out within the strict confines of the patient's relationship with the therapist. When this happens, the original neurosis can be said to have been replaced by a 'transference neurosis'.

Throughout his writings, Freud was careful to distinguish between the technique of transference analysis and the so-called 'transference cure'. This latter term is used to refer to those occasions where there is a sudden loss of symptoms due to the patient falling in love with the therapist. The dramatic superficial improvement is considered to constitute an attempt by the patient to please the psychoanalyst. This is a special phenomenon and should be considered separately.

The 'basic rule' of psychoanalysis is that the patient is required to say whatever comes into his mind, regardless of how personal, painful, fleeting or inconsequential it may seem to be. This undirected style of thinking, referred to as *free association*, is one of the means whereby the unconscious can be explored. Furthermore, because it is not reality-bound, it aids the development of transference. It should be noted that Freud did not view free association as simply random utterances, but maintained that the thought processes governing it are determined like all mentalistic events.

Dream analysis is another technique which is used to help penetrate the unconscious. When a person is asleep, defences are lowered and repressed feelings can find an outlet, albeit a symbolical one, in dreams. A dream is considered to have a *manifest* content (i.e. superficial meaning) and a *latent* content (i.e. underlying meaning). The latent content is presumed to be determined by the unacceptable motives of the individual. Thus by working on the patient's defences, as revealed through the dream contents, the therapist can help bring repressed material into the patient's consciousness and, at the same time, help to facilitate transference.

During the process of free association or dream recounting, the patient may demonstrate an unwillingness or inability to continue. This phenomenon, referred to as *resistance*, is evidenced by such behaviours as the patient suddenly 'drying up', falling asleep, changing the topic or providing a glib interpretation of an emotionally saturated occurrence. Freud (1926) isolated five different types of resistance:

1 *Repression-resistance* constitutes an attempt by the patient to prevent painful or threatening material from entering consciousness.
2 *Transference-resistance* refers to intrapsychic conflict incorporating the person of the psychoanalyst.
3 Resistance from *secondary gain* is said to occur where the patient seems reluctant to abandon the advantages provided by the illness.
4 *Id-resistance* is a term used to describe the unwillingness of the individual to consider any change in mode and form of expression of his basic instincts.
5 *Superego-resistance* refers to obstacles caused by the individual's own sense of guilt or need for punishment.

Resistances are dealt with in psychoanalysis through the process of *interpretation*. Once again there are differences of opinion as to what constitutes an interpretation. Sandler *et al.* (1970) note the arbitrariness of the distinction which some authors have made between interpretation, on the one hand, and instructions, constructions, questions, preparations for interpretation, confrontations and clarifications on the other. They suggest the following solution to this problem:

> It is fairly generally accepted in the psychoanalytic literature that no interpretation can ever be complete and perhaps the most practical use of the concept would be to include within it all comments and other verbal interventions which have the aim of making the patient aware of some aspect of his psychological functioning of which he was not previously conscious. (p. 56)

Interpretations by themselves, however, do not have any lasting effect on the patient. The various resistances which prevent insight from leading to change have to be analysed more deeply and extensively before a 'cure' can be pronounced. This aspect of psychoanalysis, known as 'working through', is considered to be an absolutely essential component of the therapeutic process. Freud (1914) claimed that the process of working through 'is a part of the work which effects the greatest changes in the patients and which distinguishes analytic treatment from any kind of treatment by suggestion'.

One factor which can apparently interfere with treatment is the manifestation of feelings which the therapist himself has for the patient. This phenomenon, known as *counter-transference*, can take the form of sadistic attacks on the patient, pompous pronouncements, suggestions of omnipotence, or overt expression of the therapist's own needs. Freud advocated that the psychoanalyst should just function like a reflecting device; conflicts which arise within the therapist are not in themselves evidence of counter-transference, and the term is just used to refer to actions which such conflicts give rise to.

The solution to this problem which Freud originally proposed was for each therapist to undergo continuous self-analysis. Because of the difficulties involved in overcoming one's own resistances, he later suggested that each psychoanalyst should undergo a 'training analysis' in order to overcome the personality deficiencies caused by unresolved conflicts. This practice is still followed in the United Kingdom. At an even later stage he claimed that this was insufficient protection against counter-transference and proposed that each analyst should be re-analysed about every five years. This recommendation, however, has rarely been followed.

Termination of therapy is considered when the patient's ego, strengthened as a result of the 'therapeutic alliance', has worked through the various unconscious feelings and attitudes, and has finally overcome the various defensive strategies it was employing. Thus, when he leaves psychoanalysis, the patient will firmly have resolved his libidinal fixations, and the energy which should formerly have been employed in psychosexual development will be liberated.

Psychoanalysis, as described above, is only available to a relatively small proportion of the population largely because of the lack of trained practitioners, and the time and expense involved. Consequently many therapists, who base their work on Freudian principles, carry out one of its derivatives, *psychoanalytically-oriented psychotherapy*. As a rule this involves one hourly session per week instead of the five or six which are required for a full analysis. In this abbreviated version of the therapeutic approach of Freud, the clinician plays a much more directive role in manipulating the transference and directing the content to those areas which are thought to be most significant. In brief psychotherapy of this sort there is a tendency for the therapist to ignore signs of disturbance which are not relevant to the presenting problems rather than to open up and work with all areas of difficulty. Thus although the free association and dream analysis techniques are occasionally employed, the fact that the focus here is on current problems means that the offering and consideration of interpretations is the more usual mode of functioning.

In *psychoanalytically-oriented group therapy* the therapist, by distancing himself, appears as an authority or 'father figure' and the members relate to each other as siblings (brothers and sisters). As in the other psychoanalytic approaches, transference and its interpretations is very basic to the whole therapeutic process. Resistance displayed by members is analysed and, in some cases at least, worked through. The group equivalent of free association is employed and dreams are interpreted in this setting as well. It is also similar to the other Freudian approaches in that therapy is carried out on a relatively long-term basis and the development of insight is considered to be more important than the removal of the 'superficial' signs of disturbance for which the patient originally sought help.

*Critical appraisal.* One of the frequently voiced criticisms of Freud from within psychoanalysis is that he overstated the role of sex in the formation of disorders of the personality. In fact his own students, Jung and Adler, broke away largely because they disagreed with the predominant position assigned to this drive in his conceptual framework. This view is shared by many contemporary psychoanalysts as well. Erikson, for instance, while not rejecting the notion of infantile sexuality, places more emphasis on the psychosocial stages of development which he claims parallel those originally elicited by Freud.

Although far less widespread, another criticism raised by psychoanalysts against Freud concerns the importance he placed on the unconscious as the prime determinant of behaviour and cognitions. Adlerians, in particular, are unimpressed by this aspect of Freud's theory and instead emphasize the 'self' which they consider to be active and conscious. Most other schools of psychoanalysis, however, share Freud's belief that the unconscious mind is a central concept in personality theory, although they have differences of opinion as to its composition and functions. Non-psychoanalysts are highly critical of the notion that all behaviour and experiences are predominantly governed by a hypothetical primitive structure which is not directly accessible.

The so-called neo-Freudians, such as Sullivan, Horney and Fromm, claim that social and cultural factors are basic to the understanding of human nature rather than the biological factors emphasized by Freud (see C3 and C5). Thus they regard such notions as the Oedipus complex and the inferiority of women as cultural and hence non-universal phenomena. They claim that even the oral and anal stages, which clearly have a large biological component, can be greatly modified by cultural factors. Consistent with this view is the work of the anthropologist Malinowski (1927), who found that in the case of the Trobriand islanders it was the maternal brother rather than the father who acted as guardian of the child. Despite the fact that this arrangement precluded the occurrence and working through of the Oedipal complex, the members of the tribe seemed remarkably free from psychiatric disorders. Thus, '... I could not name a single man or woman who was hysterical or even neurasthenic. Nervous tics, compulsory actions, or obsessive ideas were not to be found.' (Malinowski, p. 85.)

Humanists and existentialists are out of sympathy with psychoanalytic theory on the grounds that it takes a very negativistic, deterministic view of mankind. They reject out of hand the notion that the individual behaves purely in order to reduce tension resulting from pressure exerted on the ego by primitive drives. Instead they postulate that there is a positive drive for growth and development of the personality, and claim that psychological disturbances result when this is blocked in some way. This view that man is basically 'good' is in sharp contrast to the gloomy pessimism of classical Freudian theory.

Behaviourists have been particularly concerned about the fact that it is not a true scientific theory because it does not lead to the establishment of testable hypotheses capable of refutation (see A1 and A8). The main problem here is that the theory contains a number of apparently contradictory postulates which enable the psychoanalyst to account retrospectively for all eventualities. Thus passivity and dependency in adulthood can be attributed to either excessive or restricted oral gratification. Anxiety about an object or activity can lead either to the defence of *repression* (i.e. ignoring/forgetting) or *reaction-formation* (i.e. going to the opposite extreme). This latter point is well illustrated by an experiment which was carried out in order to test the link between dependency and preferred size of breasts (Scodel, 1957). The results showed that men who like women with small breasts were more dependent, as measured by the TAT. This is contrary to what might have been expected, since dependency is thought to be related to oral passivity, which in turn is thought to be connected with the individual's fixation with mammary glands. Consequently the faithful stand-by, reaction-formation, is dredged up to account for these seemingly discrepant findings. In other words it is postulated that dependent men say that they like women with small breasts because of the anxiety which they experience at the sight of large breasts, which they basically do prefer but feel they should not. It may, of course, be the case that people use different defence mechanisms in this way and that the simultaneous use of contradictory hypotheses is not merely a ploy to prevent the total collapse of the theory, as some might suspect. If this is the case, then it is up to psychoanalysts to discover the reasons for these differences so that it will prove possible to set up unidirectional hypotheses for the individual subject. To date, there has been little response to this experimental challenge. Other research projects, generally of astonishing naivety, have been carried out to defend other aspects of the psychoanalytic position and they have been critically reviewed by Kline (1972) and very critically reviewed by Eysenck (1972).

The psychoanalytic therapies have been attacked from all sides on the grounds that they attempt to force the patient into a pre-conceived theoretical structure. If he disagrees with this conceptualization of his problems and drops out of therapy then it is not the therapy which was inappropriate but the patient who is displaying 'resistance'. Once again psychoanalysis provides the answers for all occasions.

Following on from this, it must be emphasized that this model, like that of organic psychiatry, is more than just a theory and a set of techniques. It incorporates a value system. For instance it is considered 'perverse' for an individual to be dependent, homosexual or perfectionist. Thus it is possible to view the psychotherapy patient as unwittingly undertaking a course in 'brainwashing' based on the views of good and bad a particular middle-class Austrian held some fifty or so years ago.

One criticism of psychoanalysis which in fact applies to all other therapeutic approaches concerns the fact that only a limited number of people are considered 'suitable' for it. The 'YAVIS effect', which applies to all psychotherapies, refers to the finding that young, attractive, verbal, intelligent and successful people are more likely to be accepted for treatment. Other research has shown that middle-class patients tend to receive psychotherapy whereas working-class patients tend to be assigned to a behaviour therapist. These findings are particularly true so far as the psychoanalytic therapies are concerned. Although such a skewed distribution may be partially attributable to the selection bias (the seeds of counter-transference?) of the clinician, there is no doubt that this therapeutic approach is thought by its practitioners to require a reasonable intellectual level on the part of the patient and consequently some 30–40 per cent would be automatically excluded from it. It seems somewhat sinister that if some classical psychoanalysts are convinced that they alone possess the only worthwhile treatment approach, they should reserve it for 'superior' beings. Those who fall below the required standards are presumably meant to live out their unhappy lives unaided. Happily, many psychoanalysts nowadays take a more eclectic view and often consider some of the other therapies more suitable for certain patients including, occasionally, those of above average intelligence.

The final criticism levelled against psychoanalysis and associated therapies concerns the fact that their efficacy has never been unequivocally demonstrated. Eysenck (1966) has pointed out that only 67 per cent of patients who receive psychotherapy show any improvement as a result. Since he has also found that two-thirds of patients demonstrate 'spontaneous remission' (i.e. get better with no treatment), he has had to conclude that psychotherapy has not lived up to the claims that have been made for it.

There has certainly been no lack of response to such a challenging and controversial proposition. As in the case of the Rorschach, many have claimed that the relatively low rate of improvement must be attributable to the lack of experience of the therapists studied rather than to the validity of the treatment approach. The suggestion that the patients who receive therapy have probably more severe problems than those who allow two years to elapse without help has also been put forward. One of the major criticisms of Eysenck's work is that he has used the label psychotherapy to refer to all forms of verbal intervention and has drawn his conclusions from such an ill-assorted rag-bag of techniques. His response to this counter-attack is that in fact the least effective approach was found to be intensive psychoanalysis whereas a bare minimum of supportive psychotherapy was found to be the most beneficial. The work of Fiedler (1950), who showed that the length of experience of the psychotherapist is a greater determinant of psychotherapeutic outcome than whether he is a Freudian,

Adlerian or Rogerian, provides support for Eysenck's practice of looking at the efficacy of psychotherapy as a whole.

Eysenck's argument, of course, rests completely on his assertion that the rate of spontaneous remission is two-thirds. However, in a study by Paul (1966), ironically showing behaviour therapy to be more effective than psychotherapy as Eysenck would have wished, the spontaneous remission rate after two years was found to be only 22 per cent. This finding would seem to suggest that the results of psychotherapy so contemptuously dismissed by Eysenck require re-evaluation. Clearly outcome research in psychotherapy is a very complex area and at this point in time all one can say with regard to the psychoanalytic therapies is that we do not have sufficient information to reach a verdict.

## Summary and conclusions

There is no doubt that the notion of the dynamic unconscious has stirred up more controversy than any other in psychology. Differences of opinion as to its nature and function were the primary cause of the schism which developed between Freud and his students. Similarly disputes between the various psychoanalytic schools at this point in time centre around the characteristics and importance of this particular structure. From outside psychoanalysis, such seemingly disparate groups as behaviourists and humanists have joined together to reject the unconscious out of hand, though for different reasons. Nevertheless, despite the friction it has caused, the concept is still with us and, at least in Freudian circles, has undergone few modifications. The main reason why it has survived, it is claimed, is because it is so surrounded by contradictory hypotheses as to render it irrefutable. Such a state of affairs has not exactly endeared psychoanalysis to those of a scientific persuasion, and consequently this school of thought has found itself alienated from both psychology and medicine. The apparent reluctance of psychoanalysts to study the efficacy of their treatments also reflects their aversion to experimental methodology. It is hoped that, eventually, greater precision of thinking and sophistication of experimentation in this area will lead to a differentiation between the facts and the myths in Freud's writings and dispel, once and for all, the blind faith/total dismissal division which exists in psychology at present.

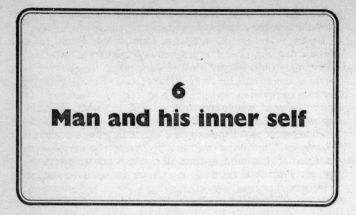

# 6
# Man and his inner self

One of the most important of the psychosocially oriented clinicians is Carl Rogers who has not only produced a theory of personality and an explanation of psychological disorders, but has introduced two very important therapeutic techniques in client-centred therapy and encounter groups. Although these two treatment approaches, at a superficial glance, seem poles apart, they are both built around the fundamental Rogerian concept of the 'self' (see D3).

A very different self theorist is R. D. Laing who found such a notion useful in helping to understand the process of so-called schizophrenia. Although in his later writings he concentrated on the role that interpersonal relationships within the family play in bringing about the schizophrenic experience, in his first important book, *The Divided Self*, he focused more on the process of 'madness' as it occurs within the individual. It is this intrapsychic model which will be considered here.

Apart from the fact that these two theorists make use of the notion of self, one other feature which they have in common is that they are both renowned critics of the medical model, with its rigid categories and crude physical remedies. Laing in fact is generally regarded as the leader of the anti-psychiatry movement in this country (see F8), although it must be said that it is very doubtful whether such a position, with its various political implications, is one that he relishes. The most striking difference between the two approaches is that whereas Rogers is almost totally interested in understanding and treating the disorders which organic psychiatrists would term 'neurotic', Laing is particularly interested in more serious breakdowns of the personality.

## Rogers' theory of the self

### General approach

Rogers takes a *phenomenological* position with regard to personality in that he holds that the reality of an object, person or situation for a particular individual is purely a function of the way it is perceived by him. He reacts according to his perception of the various phenomena surrounding him rather than to reality as defined in objective terms. Thus, according to Rogers, the only way to understand him is through his particular internal frame of reference.

A second characteristic of the Rogerian approach is that personality is regarded as a *holistic* entity. In other words the individual tends to respond as an organized totality to the events which he perceives in his phenomenal field. The notion of personality as an integrated 'whole' is a very central part of the theory.

According to Rogers, all behaviour is seen as being energized by the *actualizing tendency*, or 'the inherent tendency of the organism to develop all its capacities in ways which serve to maintain or enhance the organism' (Rogers, 1959, p. 196). This refers not only to the various psychological needs which manifest themselves but also to such psychological needs as increased autonomy and self-sufficiency. What is particularly important here is that this basic tendency serves as the criterion by which all experiences are evaluated. Those which maintain or enhance the organism are positively evaluated and therefore sought after, whereas those which have the reverse effect are judged negatively and hence avoided. The valuing process, which is specifically concerned with the psychological well-being of the individual, uses as the criterion the tendency towards *self-actualization*. Rogers' notion that the individual is motivated continuously towards the maintenance and enhancement of the self is in sharp contrast to the negativistic, tension-reducing needs as portrayed in the psychoanalytic literature.

### Theoretical rationale

Rogers (1959) postulates that each individual has a basic need to be accepted, respected and loved by significant people in his life. Whether this is innate or learned is not clear. The parent's feelings towards the child, which are not fundamentally altered at any stage despite the fact that all of the latter's behaviour is not equally approved of, is perhaps the best illustration of this. If the individual feels that other people have favourable attitudes towards him as a whole, then he will tend to engage in self-actualization behaviour rather than act out a social role. As a result of this, his 'self' will regard his experiences positively. When this happens, irrespective of how he feels about specific aspects of his behaviour, then he is said to be experiencing 'unconditional positive self-regard'.

With the possible exception of his parents and his spouse, most significant people in the individual's life make positive regard conditional upon his behaviour. To put it simply, they like him when he behaves in some ways but not when he behaves in other ways. Because the need for positive regard from such people is extremely strong, these 'conditions of worth' can supersede the system of values associated with self-actualization. Consequently the individual may end up engaging in certain experiences because other people want him to, rather than because they are maintaining or enhancing his 'self'. When this happens *threat* results.

In Rogerian theory, threat is experienced when a person perceives (or at least is dimly aware) that there is a lack of congruity between his experiences and his self-concept. It is this lack of integration which leads to the individual feeling generally uneasy and tense. Thus because of his need for positive regard, he behaves in ways which are discrepant with the values of his self and pays the price for this 'betrayal' by becoming anxious. Rogers (1959) summarizes the situation as follows:

> This, as we see it, is the basic estrangement in man. He has not been true to himself, to his own natural organismic valuing of experience, but for the sake of preserving the positive regard of others has now come to falsify some of the values he experiences and to perceive them only in terms based upon their value to others. (p. 226)

In an endeavour to reduce the threat he is experiencing, the individual makes use of the two basic defences of *denial* and *distortion*. By doing so, however, he is preventing a part of reality from being admitted to consciousness. This means that these events cannot help to shape the self-concept and the latter, as a result, becomes increasingly incongruent with reality. This in turn leads to an increase in anxiety and to an even greater use of defence mechanisms. Where the incongruence is severe and/or persistent, the individual may find that the resulting tension is interfering with his life. In the traditional classification system, such a person would be seen as suffering from a 'neurosis'. It is important to realize that although he is highly anxious through the over-use of defences, he has succeeded in keeping the self integrated, albeit somewhat tenuously. Where the inconsistency is so great as to deny distortion, the incongruent experience is accurately symbolized at a conscious level and the whole personality disintegrates. The seemingly irrational and bizarre behaviour which results is labelled 'psychotic'. Rogers claims that the behaviour in fact may be congruent with experiences which were previously denied and thus merely appear odd to the outside observer because he is not capable of perceiving events as they occur within the individual's internal frame of reference. As will be seen later, Laing's theory of 'psychosis' is somewhat similar, though far more elaborate.

*Assessment.* The basic assessment tool in Rogerian theory and therapy is the *Q-sort.* Before therapy begins, the client is given cards with statements referring to himself (e.g. 'I am a domineering person') and is asked to place them in a series of ten piles ranging from 'very characteristic of me' to 'not at all characteristic of me', according to how he views himself. When this is completed, he is asked to sort the cards again only this time in terms of his 'ideal self' (i.e. the kind of person he would like to be). The two Q-sorts are then correlated to determine the degree of discrepancy between real self and ideal self. This assessment procedure is administered at varying intervals throughout therapy in order to determine whether there is a change in the relationship between the two.

This is a good example of a case where assessment and therapy are theoretically integrated and thus where data from one can directly be carried over to the other.

*Methods of inducing change.* Rogers maintains that the threatened person can only become fully integrated again if he reduces his conditions of worth and increases his unconditional positive self-regard. Furthermore he claims that both processess are facilitated if the individual receives unconditional positive regard from a significant person in his life. Such a person must be *empathic* (i.e. able to perceive accurately the phenomenal field of the individual) before such positive regard will have any meaning for him. When the individual experiences this, he is likely to increase his own unconditional positive self-regard, reduce his use of defences, feel more integrated, and be open to new experiences. This is the basis of *client-centred therapy* (CCT) (Rogers, 1965).

In this form of treatment, the client is encouraged to direct the whole therapeutic process because it is assumed that only he can know his own unique phenomenal field. It is the therapist's task to try to learn as much as possible about the way the client views his world through empathic understanding. He does this by accepting everything the client says without demonstrating approval or disapproval. He communicates merely in order to synthesize and thus clarify feelings which the client has expressed directly or indirectly, or to reflect, but not recognize, ideas which have been expressed. Despite the fact that his role is essentially a non-directive one, the degree of change which takes place is considered to be a function of the sort of relationship he establishes with the client. Research into CCT has demonstrated that the qualities of genuineness, warmth and empathy of the therapist are very important determinants of treatment outcome (Truax and Carkhuff, 1964).

Unlike many other psychotherapists who have a humanistic flavour to their writings, Rogers has attempted to validate his theories through empirical research. In one study, Rogers and Dymond (1954) compared a group who received client-centred psychotherapy immediately, with an 'own control' group, who had to wait sixty days before receiving such treatment, and an 'equivalent control' group of people who had volunteered to take part in personality research. The purpose of this first control group was to enable a comparison to be made between changes which toow place during therapy and those which occurred during the waiting period (i.e. spontaneous remission). The second control group was included to take account of the fact that some degree of spontaneous remission might have occurred during the waiting and treatment period. The results provided support for Rogers' approach in that most change took place during therapy.

Eysenck, however, has quite correctly criticized this study on the grounds that:

(a) the waiting period for the 'own control' group was far shorter than the duration of therapy, which means that there was greater opportunity for spontaneous remission to occur during treatment;

(b) the 'equivalent control' group, which could have accounted for this time factor, is valueless because it consists of 'normals' who, by definition, are hardly likely to spontaneously remit!

This serves to illustrate how difficult it is to validate any psychotherapeutic technique.

In recent years, Rogers has moved away from individual counselling to the more directive and emotionally-charged approach of the *encounter group* (Rogers, 1970). Although his writing in this area is descriptive rather than theoretical, it would appear that the same principles as outlined above underly this treatment approach. In encounter groups the individual is encouraged (and eventually persuaded) to remove his social facade and express his feelings honestly. Essentially the group demands that each person should be himself and get in contact with his true feelings. Very often this will lead to angry confrontations between members of the group which will have to be resolved before the 'healing process' can really begin. It is important for the success of the enterprise that while the various interactions take place members provide prompt and honest feedback to each other, of both a positive and negative kind.

As a rule, after facades have been dropped and negative feelings expressed and accepted, feelings of closeness, warmth and trust develop. In theoretical terms, each individual is now receiving unconditional positive regard in that, although members may not like everything he says or does, he still receives affection from them. This enables him to reduce his conditions of worth and increase his positive self-regard. As a result he drops his use of defences, feels more integrated and becomes aware of his potential for personal growth.

Gibb (1970), in an attempt to investigate the efficacy of this approach, analysed 106 studies of encounter groups which he considered to meet scientific research requirements. From this he reached the conclusion that 'The evidence is strong that intensive group training experiences have therapeutic effects.' Many would dispute this statement on the grounds that Gibb's criteria of acceptance were very low and the findings themselves are more than a little equivocal. What is required here is well-controlled, long-term follow-up research into the effectiveness of encountering. However, the fact that the changes which are presumed to take place are mainly at an experimental level, rather than at a behavioural one, makes this a somewhat daunting task.

*Critical appraisal.* The theory itself has ben criticized on the grounds that it is unrealistic to depict man as possessing a benign inner self which is capable of limitless development, were it not for the social pressures which constrict it. Certainly it is true that Rogers does tend to minimize the role that external factors, as embodied in culture, could play in determining the direction as well as the process of self-actualization. Thus although it is obviously an attractive model of man, the almost 'soul'-like qualities of the self do not fit into everyone's picture of what human nature is all about (see D1).

CCT has been criticized on the grounds that Rogers' belief (that the therapeutic conditions are attitudinal, and that the therapist's interventions are offered in a non-selective fashion) is a mistaken one. Truax (1966), in his investigation of one of Rogers' successful cases, found that the therapist responded differently to five out of the nine categories of patient behaviour which were studied. Since the rate of emission of four out of these five classes significantly increased during therapy, it was concluded that differential reinforcement was taking place. The implication of these findings is that Rogers, despite his claims of being non-directive, is exerting control over the behaviour of his clients. This is in keeping with the behaviourist view that CCT is just a somewhat inefficient form of operant conditioning (see p. 113 and A3).

The encounter group movement has been severely attacked on the grounds that it can cause, or at least precipitate, psychological disturbances of various sorts. Many have disputed Gibb's conclusion (1970) from his research that 'there is little basis for the widespread concern among lay groups about the traumatic effects of group training'. The most systematic investigation into this area was conducted by Yalom and Lieberman (1971) who detected sixteen 'casualties' out of 209 undergraduates who had participated in encounter groups. A casualty was defined by them as:

> an individual who, as a direct result of his experience in the encounter group, became more psychologically distressed or employed more maladaptive mechanisms of defence, or both; furthermore this negative change was not a transient but an enduring one, as judged eight months after the group experience.

102

The sorts of disturbances the subjects complained of included 'psychotic' reactions, feelings of depression, withdrawal, deteriorated interpersonal relationships and general negativism and discouragement. These authors do not, however, condemn the encounter movement on the basis of these unfortunate occurrences, but make some constructive suggestions as to how high-risk subjects might be excluded. They also point out that aggressive, highly charismatic authoritarian leaders are more likely to have casualties in their groups. These findings, and the recommendations which accompany them, have been noted by the more responsible organizations who run groups, and a general 'tightening up' of patient selection and leadership training programmes has been observed in recent years. One problem about this is that with the introduction of formalization and ritualization, a lot of the evangelistic zest, which is clearly such an important component, might disappear altogether from the encounter movement.

### Laing's theory of the self

#### General approach

Like Rogers, Laing takes a phenomenological position in his attempt to understand other people, although he sees himself as an existentialist rather than as a humanist. Essentially he is concerned to regard the individual's experiences in the context of his 'being-in-the-world'. He is extremely scathing in his attack on those who take an objective detached stance in order to comprehend how human beings function:

> Depersonalization in a theory that is intended to be a theory of persons is as false as schizoid depersonalization of others and is no less ultimately an intentional act. Although conducted in the name of science, such reification yields false 'knowledge'. It is just as pathetic a fallacy as the false personalization of things. (Laing, 1960, p. 24)

In view of this belief that scientific detachment leads to alienation from the subject matter, it follows that there is no place for psychological assessment nor for statistics regarding treatment efficacy in the Laingian approach.

Since Laing's later books are in many ways inconsistent with *The Divided Self*, it is important to clarify two points at the outset. In this model, the psychotic is not depicted as a pioneer, setting out on a voyage of adventure into the unknown, as he is in the psychedelic model. Rather he emerges as someone who has failed in life, despite Laing's declared intention to avoid evaluation of anyone's being-in-the-world. The second point concerns the fact that, although he starts this book by attacking traditional psychiatry, Laing still refers to 'hysteric', 'schizoid' and 'schizophrenic' conditions as if they were syndromes. His practice of using case histories in order to illustrate unusual patterns of thinking is something he rejected by the time he had developed his family-conspirational model. It is however only his self model we are concerned with here.

## Theoretical rationale

Laing's starting point in this thesis is to define what he means by an *ontologically secure* person. Such an individual has a strong sense of his own identity, which provides him with a sound basis for encountering other people and events in his life. The ontologically insecure person, by contrast, has no such firm foundation and finds himself perpetually facing dangers which threaten his very existence. There are three types of anxiety which threaten him:

1. Engulfment – he dreads forming relationships with any-one, lest he thereby loses his identity. Rather than risk being absorbed into the other person, he prefers isolation.
2. Implosion – although in some ways he would like to fill the vacuum which is him, he is frightened to do so in case the world should 'crash in and obliterate' his identity.
3. Petrification – the idea of being 'turned to stone' by some-one else is another constant source of terror.

The thought of being partially depersonalized in a relation-ship and therefore 'a thing in the world of the other' fills him with dread.

One major characteristic of the ontologically insecure per-son is that he experiences his self as being *unembodied*. In other words, he feels detached from his physical being, unlike the embodied person who feels biologically alive. Laing illustrates this phenomenon by referring to a case who felt detached, surprised, but basically unafraid when he was as-saulted by two robbers. Being unembodied, he felt that he could not *really* be hurt by a physical attack.

For such a person, the body is just the core of the 'false self' which the detached 'inner self' regards with hatred, amusement or tenderness, as it would any other object. This 'split' is the essence of the 'schizoid' condition in Laingian theory. Direct participation in life would be to risk the inner self, and so it decides to isolate itself not only from the outside world but also from its own body. 'Participation without loss of being is felt to be impossible . . .' (Laing, ibid.).

The 'normal' person engages in a number of activities which are purely mechanical, and are therefore removed from the true self. However, in this case, not all of his behaviour is of this type, spontaneous expressions of the self can break through, and his actions are not so disparate from his self as to make him feel aware of a fundamental split between the two parts of his being. The important thing to note here is that Laing does not see the 'normal' as being qualitatively different from the other 'pathological' groups he refers to.

The 'hysteric' is depicted as someone who is attempting to achieve gratification for his inner self through his actions, but without being aware that he is so doing. In other words, the false self is helping to fulfil the inner self, although the individual denies deriving any 'gains' from his behaviour. His lack of concern about these external manifestations corresponds to the diagnostic sign of 'la belle indifférence', which appears in all orthodox psychiatric text-books (see p. 24). This is in sharp contrast to the 'schizoid' condition where the false self does not, in fact, gratify the true self. In this latter case, the self is truly unembodied.

'Schizophrenia' is seen as an extension of the schizoid condition in existential psychiatry. Laing feels that it is inevitable that the split between the true self and the non-self will eventually lead to 'psychosis'. By being so alienated, the inner self in time becomes fantasized and unreal, empty and dead, and filled with hatred and fear. According to Laing, the individual is faced with two possibilities. He can either 'be himself' completely, regardless of consequences, or 'kill' his true self to prevent it from being destroyed by others. If he attempts the first strategy, then he will give the impression to others of having suddenly 'gone mad'. The fact that the false self has been able to cope with external demands has disguised the fact that madness has been developing for some time. If he decides to kill off his very existence by denial, then he will not be able to reach other people nor they him. This will lead to withdrawal and suspiciousness. Thus whichever alternative he chooses, psychosis is the inevitable outcome.

One thing which commentators on Laing rarely emphasize

is his assertion that schizophrenia is just one possible result of the unembodied self. He claims that the split between the self and the body can lead to other outcomes which would not bring the individual into contact with a psychiatrist. He does not elaborate on this intriguing notion however.

## Methods of effecting change

Although Laing is able to construe normality, hysteria and the schizoid personality in terms of his model, so far as intervention is concerned he has worked almost exclusively with schizophrenia. The aim of therapy, in this latter case, is to remove the split which is presumed to exist between the real self and the false selves. The traditional psychiatric hospital, according to Laingians, is the last place on earth to help him reach such a state of integration. Chemotherapy combined with the rigid routine of the institution merely serves to restore the status quo between the true and false selves, in their opinion. Orthodox psychiatrists, as such, are seen to be dehumanizing the patient by labelling him 'mad', instead of attempting to understand his way of experiencing reality.

In place of the mental institution, Laing advocates a type of therapeutic community where the individual can be helped to achieve intrapsychic union rather than have his whole integration process arrested. Kingsley Hall, in London's east end, was the first establishment created specifically for treatment along the lines of existential psychiatry. In order to illustrate the precise nature of treatment in this alternative psychiatry setting, a brief summary of Laing's most celebrated case, Mary Barnes, is provided. This is based on the report by Gordon (1971).

Mary was diagnosed as schizophrenic in 1953 and was placed in a mental hospital for a year. When she was discharged, she took a job as a nursing tutor in a general hospital and managed to cope with this sort of life for several years. By 1963 she had become aware that her whole existence was in fact a complete facade, and sought help from Laing. She expressed to him a desire to return to a pre-natal state and develop all over again. As soon as Kingsley Hall opened, Mary was invited to move in and live through this experience. After a few weeks in this setting, she began the process of regression and, before long, was unable to eat solid foods and had to be bottle-fed. Several crises then followed which placed great strain on the community. At one stage she stopped sucking, urinating and defecating, and appeared to be returning to a womb-like state. At another time she upset members by smearing faeces on the walls. Whenever there was a crisis of this sort, the members of the community would meet in order to discuss what course of action to take. Everyone was thus intimately involved in Mary's 'journey'. Eventually she started to progress through childhood and played the sorts of games she had never been allowed to as a little girl. Apart from a slight relapse in 1966, she made steady progress and was soon behaving in a more adult-like manner.

## Critical appraisal

Probably no psychiatrist since Freud has captured the imagination of the educated lay person as Laing has done. The young radicals hail him as a Messiah of the Left, and attribute a lot of socialist beliefs to him which can certainly be read into his work, but which have never been explicitly stated by him. For many others, he is just the embodiment of their belief that treating psychiatric patients as lists of symptoms is a socially degrading procedure.

Orthodox psychiatrists and psychologists, on the other hand, regard his writings to be interesting but largely irrelevant. When confronted with his work, they make the following points. Drugs have been found to be effective in treating schizophrenics, particularly those with a poor pre-morbid background (Goldstein et al., 1969). It should be noted, however, that in medically-oriented psychiatry, schizophrenia is indicated by the presence of signs rather than of symptoms. Laingians would claim that what has happened in such cases is that the individual's false self is now operating again, while the fundamental split between the true and false selves is still present. Thus, although according to external criteria he has improved, from an existential-phenomenological viewpoint he is still ontologically insecure.

Orthodox psychiatrists are also quick to point out that the majority of Laing's schizophrenics had good pre-morbid personalities. Research has shown that such people tend to improve after an 'episode', regardless of the type of therapy they receive. Spontaneous remission is in fact observed in many cases. The strength of this argument lies in the fact that existential psychiatrists are indeed highly selective in the sorts of patients they will accept into their therapeutic communities.

Scientifically oriented clinicians are critical of the fact that his models cannot be stated as hypotheses, and thus subjected to experimentation. Similarly it is pointed out that the efficacy of the Kingsley Hall project itself has never been unequivocally demonstrated, because of the complete absence of objective measures and control groups. Laing, of course, feels that such research is quite pointless and could even be harmful since, by its very nature, it depersonalizes the person.

Thus, in order to get involved in existential psychiatry, one has got to be able to tolerate quite a considerable amount of ambiguity. This is not a particularly striking characteristic of those who have graduated from our various clinical training courses, where the emphasis is very much on reducing diverse material to a simple, manageable form.

## Summary and conclusions

The theories of Rogers and Laing have many features in common. Both reject the traditional psychiatric approach of regarding the individual objectively, in favour of the phenomenological approach with its emphasis on the patient's actual experiences. They both see man's distress as emanating from a division between his real self and the self which interacts with others. So far as intervention is concerned, humanists and existentialists agree on the fact that a safe and supportive atmosphere should be provided to help the individual unearth and overcome his various anxieties.

One difference between the two concerns the precise nature of the anxieties which threaten the inner self. For Laing, the individual is terrified lest the world should break in and depersonalize him, whereas Rogerian man experiences distress because he is not behaving in a way which would maintain or enhance the self. In other words, for Laing anxiety emanates from without, whereas for Rogers it comes from within. This could be a reflection of the fact that Rogers is primarily interested in 'neurotic' disorders whereas 'psychosis' is the focal point of Laingian theory.

Perhaps the most fundamental difference between the two is that whereas Laing is primarily a philosopher, Rogers is very much a psychologist first and a philosopher second. Thus he makes use of assessment procedures and encourages research into the effectiveness of his types of therapy. For Laing, clinical research is not only dehumanizing for the individual but is also completely irrelevant so far as understanding the person is concerned. Both however have made very important contributions to the psychosocial movement.

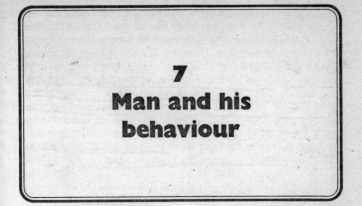

# 7
# Man and his behaviour

Behavioural therapy is that approach to the treatment of psychiatric disorders which 'denotes the use of experimentally established principles of learning for the purpose of changing unadaptive behaviour' (Wolpe, 1968, p. 557). Although the term was first introduced by Skinner to refer to operant conditioning work with psychotics (see p. 119), the emergence of the school of behaviour therapy as an entity is normally associated with Eysenck. Not content with developing the new therapeutic approach, however, Eysenck attempted to enhance the reputation of the new treatment school by attacking the other psychological therapies. Thus, according to his way of thinking, 'psychotherapy itself, when shorn of its inessential and irrelevant parts, can usefully be considered as a minor part of behaviour therapy' (Eysenck, 1960, p. ix).

Although extensive contributions have been made by such psychiatrists as Wolpe and Marks, the field of behaviour therapy has been dominated largely by clinical psychologists. This is largely due to the fact that psychologists are generally better acquainted with the underlying theoretical principles and are therefore better able to apply them. It is important to realize that, despite the apparent simplicity of this approach, a thorough knowledge of basic facts about learning is essential for the proper use of behavioural techniques. Certainly many of the disappointing results obtained by psychiatrists in the 1960s can be attributed to their failure to incorporate the knowledge, acquired experimentally, about learning processes, into their treatment approaches.

Thus it is important to make it clear at the outset that a

superficial understanding of the techniques presented in this chapter is insufficient in itself to enable the untrained clinician to start practising behaviour therapy.

*General approach*

Behaviourists consider the majority of psychiatric disorders to be purely maladaptive forms of responding which have been acquired as a result of traumatic or inappropriate conditioning experiences. In contrast to all the other psychosocial schools, they do not view behavioural abnormalities as mere signs of intrapsychic disturbance. Instead they maintain that if you 'get rid of the symptom ... you have eliminated the neurosis' (Eysenck, 1960, p. 9). Since they reject the notion of 'underlying causes', it follows that they too reject the notion of mental illness. Their reasons for so doing, however, are different from those of the psychoanalysts, humanists and existentialists. These three groups adopt the medical viewpoint that disturbances at a superficial level are 'symptomatic' of the basic problems, but do not agree with organic psychiatrists that individuals can usefully be slotted into specific disease categories. Behaviourists, on the other hand, while dismissing the idea of deep-seated mental 'pathology' have made more than a little use of the neo-Kraepelinian classification system.

There are many differences between behavioural therapy and the other psychotherapies which follow on from this fundamental difference of opinion regarding cause. Behaviourists reject out of hand the view that 'insight' has to be achieved before any effective change can take place, although they will concede that 'awareness' of stimulus-response connections can facilitate the learning process. They concentrate much more on the individual's current situation than on his past history, although knowledge of significant events in his life can sometimes be used in helping to design treatment programmes. They regard the patient-therapist relationship to be useful only inasmuch as the therapist will be a more effective 'positive reinforcer' (i.e. rewarding agency) if the patient likes him. Thus the patient may be more inclined to try to change his behaviour in order to gain the approval of a therapist whom he evaluates highly. Behaviour therapists are far more directive than other therapists but, at the same time, generally encourage the patient to play an active role and take on a lot of the responsibility for change. Thus patients are invited to become involved in devising the treatment programme and deciding on practical assignments which they must carry out if any real change is to occur.

Finally it must be pointed out that, contrary to the common stereotype, behaviour therapy is not a unitary concept. In the last few years a gap has developed, and is gradually widening, between those who take a nomothetic position and those who follow an idiographic line. The former group stick rigidly to the formal classification system and devote their research energies to discovering which set of techniques is most effective with each of the diagnostic groups. Eysenck, Rachman and Marks are among the most celebrated proponents of this viewpoint. The idiographic behaviourists are critical of this approach because it is too closely allied to a rigid, invalid and alien conceptual system, because it favours crude 'package deal' type therapy, and because it is associated with the value system of organic psychiatry. Instead they propose that behaviourists should attempt to isolate the stimuli and consequences which are maintaining the inappropriate behaviour in the individual case, and that the treatment programme should be derived from a 'behavioural analysis' of this type. Yates and Meyer are just two of the names associated with the view that behaviour therapy should be geared to the individual rather than to the diagnostic group. Since the ways of arriving at treatment decisions is so different for these groups, they will be discussed separately in the section on methods of effecting change, under the arbitrary headings of behavioural technology and behavioural psychotherapy respectively.

*Theoretical rationale*
Although, as has been pointed out, behaviour therapists can be divided into two main camps, there are many more divisions of opinion regarding the precise theoretical explanations of the development of psychiatric disorders. It is clearly outside the scope of this book to do any more than hint at some of the areas of dispute, and the reader is referred to Bandura (1969) for a comprehensive review of this whole field.

'Neurotic' disorders, by and large, are considered to arise through a process of *Pavlovian* or *classical conditioning* (see A3). Essentially what happens is that a neutral object, by being paired with an anxiety-arousing stimulus, becomes a source of anxiety itself. In conditioning jargon, the term for the originally neutral object is the *conditioned stimulus* (CS), the original source of anxiety is known as the *unconditioned stimulus* (UCS), and the anxiety itself is called the *unconditioned response* (UCR). The two important features to note about this form of conditioning are that the organism is passive throughout, and that the model is limited to dealing with autonomic patterns of response (e.g. anxiety, salivation, sexual arousal).

The classic case of the eleven-month-old boy, Little Albert (Watson and Raynor, 1920) provides a clear illustration of how a phobia can be created through classical conditioning. Quite simply, Albert developed a 'phobia' of white rats after one had been paired on several occasions with a loud noise, caused by striking an iron bar. In this study, the rat is the CS, the noise the UCS, and the anxiety the UCR. In keeping with Pavlov's principle of response generalization, Albert also displayed anxiety in the presence of other furry animals as a result of the experiment. Since the 'phobia' persisted for over a month, it is claimed by behaviourists to be analogous to the 'neurotic fears' observed in the clinic.

Classical conditioning is also assumed to play an important part in determining sexual orientation. An experiment conducted by Rachman (1966) demonstrates how fetishism can be created in the laboratory by means of this particular learning paradigm. A photograph of a pair of black, knee-length boots (CS) was repeatedly shown just before slides of sexually provocative nudes (UCS). Before the experiment began, it had been demonstrated that penile volume increased (UCR) in response to the nudes but not to the boots. As a result of the association which built up between the two types of stimuli, the subjects learned eventually to respond sexually to the picture of the boots. The response also generalized to other types of women's footwear.

One serious limitation of the classical conditioning paradigm is that whereas it may explain how phobias and sexual deviations can arise, it cannot explain why they continue over time. One of Pavlov's important findings was that, if the CS is presented on a number of occasions without the UCS, then the CS will gradually lose its arousing properties until eventually complete *extinction* of the response takes place (see A3). Why is it, therefore, that phobias persist? The answer to this question is twofold. In the first place there is evidence (e.g. Eysenck and Rachman, 1965) that the majority of conditioned anxiety responses do extinguish eventually (spontaneous recovery). The second part of the answer takes account of the fact that there is one crucial difference between Pavlov's dog and the man in the street: the man can choose not to go into situations which would facilitate extinction, whereas the harnessed laboratory animal is denied such a choice. The learning paradigm for understanding voluntary behaviour of this sort is called instrumental or *operant conditioning*, and is associated with the work of Skinner.

In operant conditioning, the subject learns that if he responds in the presence of a specific stimulus (called the *discriminative stimulus* (or SD)), then this behaviour will be followed by a particular consequence. Since whether he makes this response or not depends on the antecedent conditions, it is customary to state that the stimulus is therefore exerting control over his behaviour (i.e. *stimulus control*). According to Skinner, there are three types of consequence of a response. *Positive reinforcement* (reward) is an outcome which will lead to an increase in the rate of emission. *Punishment* brings about a decrease in the frequency of occurrence of that behaviour. The third, and most interesting in this context, is called *negative reinforcement*. This refers to the situation where the removal of a noxious stimulus leads to an increase in response rate. Negative reinforcement is involved in *avoidance conditioning*, where the subject's response prevents the unpleasant occurrence, and in *escape conditioning*, where the response terminates it after it has begun.

Going back to the original question of why phobias persist, the answer, so far as many behaviourists are concerned, lies in the fact that the patient can avoid and/or escape from anxiety-provoking situations, thus preventing the process of extinction from taking place. If he were to remain in the situation, the anxiety would eventually disappear. The negative reinforcement which is maintaining this behaviour is simply the removal of anxiety. Thus a two-factor learning model is utilized to explain the genesis and the persistence of specific anxiety responses. They arise through classical conditioning and are maintained by the operant behaviour of the individual.

Since the avoidance and the escape responses are so strongly reinforced, there is always the possibility that they might become more extensive and elaborate. It is conjectured that the bizarre behaviour patterns which result could lead to the individual developing what is traditionally referred to as an 'obsessive-compulsive' disorder. Thus, for instance, the

113

excessive hand-washer might in fact be a 'dirt phobic' who is continuously engaged in avoidance rituals to reduce this source of anxiety. What is not clear from the behaviour therapy literature is why some people just avoid anxiety-eliciting situations, whereas others go on to develop elaborate, precautionary sequences of behaviour.

The two-factor model of learning is also required to explain why sexual 'deviations' arise and persist. As has already been shown by reference to the Rachman experiment, classical conditioning can account for the way in which a neutral object becomes invested with sexually arousing properties. In this case, the instrumental behaviour which prevents extinction from taking place and which strengthens the association is the act of masturbation. When the individual engages in this positively reinforcing activity, he makes use of the most sexually arousing fantasy available to him. Thus if he is masturbating soon after a 'deviant' classical conditioning occurrence, then he is likely to employ a fantasy centred around that situation. As he repeatedly masturbates to this fantasy as his exclusive sexual outlet, the erotic value of the deviant fantasy gradually increases. Eventually he finds himself unable to become sexually aroused unless he is using this particular fantasy. Thus classical conditioning can account for the onset of the deviation and for its augmentation through masturbation, while the act of masturbation itself recurs as a result of operant conditioning. McGuire et al. (1965) present a number of case histories to illustrate this process.

A totally different behavioural model, derived from experimental work with animals, has recently been proposed to account for the development of 'depression' (Seligman, 1973). When a person is placed in a noxious environment where no responses are negatively reinforced, he will eventually stop responding and become totally passive. What is particularly interesting about this is that this 'learned helplessness' is not situation-specific. Thus when placed in another environment where reinforcement is available, he will still not respond. In other words he has learned that responding is just not worth the effort. It will be recalled that lack of energy is one of the clinical features of 'depression'. Similarly, an individual will learn to be helpless if he gets rewarded regardless of what he does. An example of this is the pop-star who is lavishly praised whether his performance merits it or not. After a while he stops responding and becomes 'depressed'. To summarize, Seligman is proposing that 'reactive depression' results when reinforcers are not made contingent upon responding.

From the above examples it will be apparent that behaviourists have been quite ingenious in conceptualizing seemingly complex behaviour in terms of two experimentally-derived models of learning. Since they have demonstrated, to their own satisfaction at least, that disorders are caused by relatively simple mechanistic occurrences, it follows that the treatments they have devised are equally uncomplicated and free from intangibles. Furthermore their assessment techniques are employed purely to describe and measure behaviour, rather than to delve into such nebulous areas as the self and the unconscious.

*Assessment procedures.* Behaviourists, with the notable exception of Eysenckians (see D3), have found little place for personality questionnaires or other standardized assessment procedures in their clinical work. As Mischel (1968) pointed out, the behavioural correlates of personality traits are very much in doubt. True, some behaviourists make use of questionnaires which have been developed specifically to help pin-point problem areas. The Geer Fear Schedule (Geer, 1965) is an example of such a potentially time-saving device. Nevertheless, except in the case of large-scale research projects, behaviourists have found little use for global assessment techniques. Instead they are more concerned to collect information which has been derived from observations of behaviour. The ways of doing this range from painstakingly precise laboratory observations to diary-keeping by the patient.

The most valid form of assessment is considered to be behavioural sampling of the individual's responses in naturalistic settings. As a rule this simply involves obtaining frequency counts of the desired behaviours by just adding up the total emitted, or by observing at fixed intervals (time-sampling). Although this sounds fairly straightforward, there are certain methodological problems which can be partially reduced if the following four precautions are taken:

1. The specific behaviours must be clearly defined.
2. The observers should be trained to recognize these behaviours, in order to increase scoring reliability.
3. The behaviours must be described as discrete events, to facilitate observation and recording.

115

4. Simple data sheets or event recorders should be provided to reduce time spent actually recording.

Other difficulties include the risk of observer bias and the effect on the subject of being observed. Lipinski and Nelson (1974) review these and other problems associated with naturalistic observation.

The majority of clinicians, however, do not have teams of trained observers on hand to help them carry out such sophisticated procedures, and have to make do with much cruder ones. These include 'behavioural tests', such as taking the 'agoraphobic' (see p. 20) for a walk or the unassertive person to a social situation, which give the therapist a clearer idea of the problem. Another useful device is simply to ask the patient to keep a note of the number of times he carries out a piece of behaviour each day. The advantage of these forms of assessment, unsystematic as they most certainly are, is that they are directly linked to treatment. Because both therapy and assessment are theoretically compatible, the information from one can be easily carried over to the other. As has been emphasized throughout this book, clinical assessment is completely irrelevant if it does not provide information which can be incorporated directly into the mode of intervention.

*Methods of effecting change.* As intimated earlier in this chapter, it is possible to make a distinction between behavioural 'technologists' and behavioural 'psychotherapists'. Since the differences in their approaches are quite marked, it will be useful to consider them separately.

*Behavioural technology*
Behavioural technologists have allied themselves closely to the formal diagnostic categories, and have endeavoured to devise techniques for each of these 'syndromes'. Because of the non-specialist nature of this book, it is possible only to mention briefly some of the more common behavioural modes of intervention.

By far the greatest amount of space in the behaviour therapy literature is devoted to 'neurotic' disorders, and 'phobias' in particular. The first important break-through in this field was achieved by Wolpe (1958), who devised a technique called *systematic desensitization* for the treatment of specific anxiety responses. Preparatory to treatment, the patient is asked to list the various situations in which he experiences anxiety in hierarchical order. He is then requested to imagine the least anxiety-provoking situation while carrying out a 'response antagonistic to anxiety' (Wolpe, 1958). This can either be an assertive act, or, more usually, muscular relaxation. Should he be able to do this without experiencing anxiety, then the next item is presented and the whole process is repeated. Treatment is continued until he can imagine the situation at the top of the hierarchy without feeling anxious. The basic rule in desensitization is that, should the patient become tense at any stage, he should indicate this to the therapist who will then ask him to think about a situation lower down the hierarchy. The difficult item will be tackled again after he has received more preparatory training. The rationale behind this is that if the patient experiences anxiety while thinking about a particular situation, then the association between the CS and the UCR will be strengthened. Finally it should be noted that patients can also be desensitized in real-life situations ('in vivo').

Another much-used behavioural treatment for 'phobias' is entitled *implosive therapy* (Stampfl and Levis, 1967). This is based on the view that extinction of conditioned anxiety responses will take place if the patient can be prevented from carrying out avoidance or escape manoeuvres. In this case the patient is asked to imagine himself in the most anxiety-provoking situation he can. Since it is presumed that the speed of extinction is very much a function of the intensity of the stimulation, the therapist continually provides additional cues and images in order to maximize the patient's anxiety. Eventually, despite all the efforts of the therapist, the patient's anxiety level falls. The treatment session is terminated when he is imagining the worst possible situation while feeling free from tension. The bond between the CS and the UCR is presumed to have weakened as a result of this. A similar technique is *flooding* which also involves prolonged exposure, though usually in the 'in vivo' situation. The basic difference between the two is that, in flooding, the therapist takes the patient to his most feared situation but does not engage in stimulus augmentation. In both cases it is imperative that the session is continued until the anxiety level has dropped, otherwise no extinction will take place.

Where the anxiety is 'free-floating', or in instances where the individual has many conditioned anxiety responses, behaviourists prefer *anxiety management* training to the above techniques. This involves asking the patient to imagine himself in an anxiety-eliciting situation and then, at a command, to relax himself. To facilitate the latter process, it is customary to attach the patient to a 'bio-feedback' machine (see A2), which gives him precise information as to his state of 'arousal' at any moment in time. This training procedure is repeated many times until the patient has adequately developed the skills involved in controlling anxiety.

With 'obsessional-compulsive' disorders, *ritual prevention* is very much the treatment of choice. It is assumed that by stopping these avoidance and escape responses, the anxiety will come to the surface where it can be dealt with by the above methods. Although this is the theoretical rationale behind the approach, there are mixed reports as to whether anxiety does in fact become more pronounced as a result of the prevention of the obsessive behaviour. While this procedure has been found to be useful in eliminating undesired behavioural habits, it has by no means been always the case that associated repetitive thoughts have disappeared as well. Thus various techniques have been developed to deal with maladaptive cognitive responses of this kind. In *thought-stopping*, the patient is asked to dwell on his irrational and futile preoccupations and while so doing is suddenly interrupted by the cry of 'Stop' from his therapist. Immediately afterwards he is made aware that the thought processes have indeed terminated as a result. The process is repeated with the patient shouting the command. Eventually, when he has learned to do this subvocally, he is considered to be capable of exerting control over these deviant thoughts in the real-life situation. In *blow-up* therapy, the patient is encouraged to embellish his ruminations until they are so far-fetched that he has to dismiss them all on grounds of total irrationality.

Another large area into which behaviour therapists have made impressive advances is that of sexual 'deviations'. The early work on this topic has centred largely around the controversial practice of *aversion therapy*. This generally involves the simultaneous presentation of pictorial stimuli, associated with the particular deviation in question and a noxious stimulus (usually electric shock). As a result of this traumatic conditioning procedure, the individual typically finds that the sexually-arousing properties surrounding this outlet have greatly diminished. Although it sounds very straightforward, the actual mode of presentation is very much a function of the learning paradigm adopted. The clinical research of Feldman and MacCulloch (1965) would seem to suggest that the more sophisticated anticipatory avoidance conditioning (see p. 113) is superior to classical conditioning, although not everyone has agreed with this interpretation of their results (Rachman and Teasdale, 1969).

In recent years, an alternative to aversion therapy called *covert sensitization* (Cautela, 1967) has grown in popularity. This simply involves getting the patient to imagine himself in his favoured sexual situation, while the therapist provides an anxiety-provoking commentary. Although less precise than aversion therapy procedures, many behaviour therapists prefer to use it on humanitarian grounds.

As a rule, behaviour therapists make use of techniques to increase heterosexual interests as well as (or even instead of) either of these two approaches. Masturbatory fantasy retaining programmes of various sorts have been developed to help the individual change his sexual orientation. More structured classical and operant conditioning programmes have also been found to be effective in increasing the erotic value of heterosexual stimuli for sexual deviants. These more constructive approaches certainly make a welcome relief from the essentially negativistic work which has dominated this field for so long.

A very different sort of behaviour therapy has been employed in the everyday management of wards occupied by 'schizophrenics'. This approach, known as the *token economy* system (Ayllon and Azrin, 1968), is essentially a training programme based on principles of operant conditioning. Reinforcing activities (e.g. watching TV) are made contingent on the performance of 'target' behaviours. Because it is imperative that reinforcement should follow the desired response immediately, the patients are assigned tokens as soon as they have completed a task. These tokens can be exchanged at a later stage for the special privileges. Although it has been shown quite unequivocally that such programmes lead to an increase in target behaviours, the generalization of the responses to the outside world is more open to question.

These are just some of the problem areas which have been tackled by behaviour therapists. Advances have also been made in such diverse areas as sexual dysfunction, gambling, speech disorders, subnormality, alcoholism, autism, psychogeriatrics and obesity. Unlike most other therapists, behavioural technologists have been very concerned to carry out exhaustive research projects into each new technique as it is developed. This means that the clinician who later employs them, does so confident in the knowledge that they have been tried and tested.

*Behavioural psychotherapy*. Many behaviour therapists, while appreciating the research carried out by their technologist colleagues, disapprove of their close alliance to the traditional diagnostic categories. For them, as for Rogerians and Freudians, the individual should be the object of study in his own right. Although they make use of the same devices as the technologists, the ones they employ in any particular case is determined by the 'behavioural analysis' they carry out rather than by the category he would appear to belong to. In their view, the 'phobic', who only receives sympathy from her spouse when talking about her anxieties, would derive little real benefit from desensitization. Aversion therapy would be of little help to the alcoholic who drinks because he is socially inadequate. Certainly in many cases the answer would be the same as that suggested by the diagnosis, but in many others the behavioural analysis would lead to a quite different treatment approach being adopted.

The main steps involved in behavioural analysis are as follows:

1. Define exactly the problem behaviours.
2. Determine the environmental conditions (SD) which alter the frequency of the behaviour.
3. Isolate the reinforcers which maintain the behaviour.
4. Attempt to link up the problem areas as a result of this knowledge.
5. Test out hypotheses by asking specific questions about the patient's past history.
6. Re-test the hypotheses by implementing a treatment programme.
7. Revise hypotheses and treatment as and when required.

Recently, Frankel (1975) has suggested that the analysis should be extended even further in order to take account of response chains which operate between other members of the individual's social milieu.

The appeal of behavioural psychotherapy lies in the fact that the techniques it employs have been well-researched, combined with the fact that it is flexible and individualistic. The danger however is that its practitioners, in their endeavour to dissociate themselves from the 'hard-liners', might find themselves in the end practising unstructured, woolly counselling, of a non-interpretive nature.

*Critical appraisal*

Despite the apparent scientific respectability of behaviour therapy, it has been severely attacked on the grounds that its techniques bear only a tenuous resemblance to the principles from which they have been derived (Breger and McGaugh, 1965). It has been pointed out by these authors that, so far as desensitization is concerned, the stimulus of 'imagination of a scene' and the response of 'relaxation' are 'only remotely allegorical to the traditional use of these terms in psychology'. They quarrel with the assumption that the whole treatment approach is based on 'modern learning theory' by pointing out that there is no general agreement as to how rats learn to run mazes, never mind how humans develop psychological disturbances. Regarding the efficacy of the techniques, these authors point out flaws in the designs of some of the early experiments and conclude that 'most of the claims ... must be regarded as no better substantiated than those of any other enthusiastic school of psychotherapy whose practitioners claim that their patients get better'. Although the improved quality of research in recent years would lead one to dispute the latter point, there is no doubt that many of Breger and McGaugh's other arguments still carry a lot of weight.

Psychoanalytic writers have always been critical of the 'symptomatic' nature of behaviour therapy and have stated quite categorically that such a superficial approach must inevitably lead to 'symptom substitution' (i.e. creation of another problem). Empirical research, however, has not suggested that there is any greater risk of this happening with behaviour therapy than with other therapies. The main problem here is in defining what constitutes a new symptom, and stipulating its relationship to the old one. Ironically it is the behavioural psychotherapists, nowadays, who have become particularly sensitive regarding their issue. In many cases they would in fact predict that the removal of a response, while leaving the relevant SD untouched, must lead to the formation of another maladaptive response. Logical though their arguments may be, one is still left with the research findings that there is no particular risk of new symptoms following even the most technological variety of behaviour therapy. This area is well reviewed by Cahoon (1968).

Finally, behaviour therapy has been criticized on the

grounds that it may work with simple tangible problems, but it can do little for the great bulk of non-specific problems which present in the psychiatric clinic. Although there was a lot of truth in this argument up to ten years or so ago, recent developments which have taken place in this field would suggest that such allegations are unwarranted. One outstanding example here is the work of Meichenbaum (1973) who has developed an approach for directly modifying the patient's cognitive responses (i.e. what he tells himself). Such techniques are particularly useful in those cases where there are few behavioural signs of disturbance, and where distress is caused mainly by maladaptive thoughts. Research findings such as this would suggest that it would be premature at this stage to pronounce a final judgement on behaviour therapy regarding range of application.

## Summary and conclusions

For a comparatively young treatment school, there is no doubt that behaviour therapy has proved itself successful with a wide assortment of clinical problems. One indirect result of the proven efficacy of its techniques is that grave doubts have now been cast on the necessity of maintaining such nebulous concepts as the 'self' and the 'unconscious'. This has led to other psychotherapists being stimulated into carrying out research projects in an endeavour to justify the continued use of their fundamental concepts. Such research is most welcome in a field which has stagnated for so long.

Although behaviour therapy was very unpopular for a time in both lay and learned circles, mainly on account of the crudity of aversion techniques and the rigidity of its conceptual system, there are signs that opinion is changing. The recent arousal of interest into cognitive processes is seen as a very welcome development. The flexible, but still rigorous, sub-school of behavioural psychotherapy is another. Perhaps the most important contribution of all to this change in climate concerns the fact that behaviour therapists are now more concerned to develop their own approach than to criticize those of their psychotherapeutic colleagues.

Finally, however, it still remains to be seen how much behaviour therapists can achieve in this field with just their two simple models of learning.

# 8
# Man and his conceptual system

The Personal Construct Theory (PCT) of George Kelly has made a considerable impact on clinical psychology in this country, largely as a result of the evangelistic zeal of its principal devotee, Donald Bannister. The general approach is quite similar to that of Rogers in that the individual is considered to be the most knowledgeable person with regard to his own unique problems. In view of this, he is encouraged to divulge all relevant information to the therapist, rather than for the therapist to attempt to infer the 'real' nature of these problems from his words and deeds, as in the psychoanalytic schools. In other words, for Kelly, man is considered to be perfectly rational and should be treated as such.

Since PCT has been described in some depth elsewhere (F1), the emphasis here will be very much on the attempts which have been made to apply this model to the understanding, assessment, and treatment of psychological disturbances. It should be pointed out that Kelly himself was not particularly concerned to extend his theory to incorporate all types of psychiatric disorders, and it has been left largely to Bannister and his colleagues to fill this particular gap.

*General approach.* In PCT, man is portrayed as a scientist who is constantly engaged in making sense out of his world. He sets up hypotheses, tests them out by behaving, and hopefully alters his theory on the basis of these results. Since each individual has his own unique conceptual system, no two people can perceive or react to situations in exactly the same way. As in academic life, however, some people make better scientists than others. Some use blinkers and operate strictly within narrow confines where they know their predictions will be confirmed. Others devise such imprecise and untestable theories that they are unable to make any predictions at all. The aim of construct therapy, therefore is, in a sense, to make the individual more conversant with research methodology, so that he will be able to build for himself a flexible, but manageable, theory concerning the functioning of objects in his own personal environment.

*Theoretical rationale.* According to Kelly, each person views and interprets his world through bi-polar concepts called *constructs* (e.g. good-bad; kind-cruel) which enable him to predict events. These constructs are depicted as being systematically organized in a pyramidal fashion, with the individual's *superordinate* (i.e. most important) constructs at the top. This cognitive structure is continually undergoing change as the individual interacts with the ever-changing objects in his environment. Its precise nature at any particular point in time is considered to be a function of the outcome of the individual's various predictions about his world.

Each prediction he makes, with the constructs at his disposal, leads to one of three possible outcomes. If the particular element behaves in a manner which has been anticipated, the constructs used can be said to have been *validated*. If the outcome is not what was expected, then the constructs are considered to have been *invalidated*. The third possibility is that the element may turn out to be *outside the range of convenience* of the constructs, in that the evidence may neither support nor disconfirm the predictions. In line with reinforcement principles, constructs which are consistently validated tend to be maintained, whereas those which are invalidated tend to be used less frequently. Furthermore, since the individual is concerned to make as much sense out of his world as he can, he will endeavour to ensure that the range of convenience of his constructs is wide enough to help him cope with all elements he is likely to encounter.

One of Kelly's own constructs is that peoples' systems can be either 'tight' or 'loose'. This is determined by means of the repertory grid technique (p. 126). A tight construct system is one which leads to strong, definite predictions, whereas a loose system gives rise to varying predictions. Both extreme positions have their advantages and disadvantages. The tight construer, with his clear-cut expectations, is able to make sense out of his limited world with ease. However, at the same time, he runs the risk of having his constructs invalidated. The loose construer, on account of the variable nature of his precepts, does not meet with such unambiguous failure but, on the other hand, feels hopelessly confused about his highly complex world.

The tightness-looseness idea is very central to Bannister's theories as to the nature of the various types of psychological disturbances. On the basis of the theory, one might predict that 'neurotics' would have tight inflexible systems. Their anxiety could then be attributed to the fact that so many daily occurrences occur outside the range of convenience of their constructs. Furthermore, the fact that their constructs would be being invalidated regularly would lead them to use defence mechanisms in order to distort the incoming evidence, and thus avoid the necessity of changing their theories about the world. The evidence, however, is not entirely consistent with this hypothesis. For instance, although Bannister *et al.* (1971) found that 'neurotics' had tighter systems than alcoholics, depressives and organics, there was found to be no difference between 'neurotics' and 'normals' when the Bannister-Fransella test was standardized.

The situation has been somewhat clarified by work that has been carried out with 'obsessionals' (e.g. Makhlouf-Norris *et al.*, 1970). Contrary to what might have been expected, 'obsessionals' have been found to have very loose systems with one or two disconnected 'constellations' (i.e. clusters of intercorrelated constructs) which refer to their ruminations and compulsive behaviours. It is conjectured that in view of the looseness of the remainder of their systems, they tend to function within the tight areas, which at least help them to make some sense out of their world. Such findings concerning the non-homogeneity of the 'neurotic' population strongly support the arguments raised in Part 1 concerning the clinical uselessness of the major diagnostic categories.

The theory might also lead one to expect that the confusion exhibited by thought-disordered 'schizophrenics' could be attributed to the fact that they are operating with loose construct systems. This hypothesis has been strongly confirmed many times and, in fact, the Bannister-Fransella test was constructed on the basis of these findings. Bannister (1963) has attempted to account for the genesis of this looseness in terms of *serial invalidation*. It is argued that if a person's construc-

125

tion of an element is repeatedly invalidated, then he will initially attempt to deal with this by switching the person or object from pole to pole. For example, mother may be seen as being loving, then hating, then loving again, all in the space of a few hours. Eventually he will be forced to weaken the relationship between this construct and the others in his system. If this process recurs with several of his constructs, then he will find himself eventually operating with a set of loosely constructed predictive constructs which do not enable him to make sense out of his environment. Thus while the 'normal' construer might expect a 'loving' person to be 'honest', 'trustworthy' and 'genuine', the loose construer would be unable to make such predictions. It is postulated, therefore, that the schizophrenic is someone who has been forced to loosen up his constructs because of contradictory evidence. This has led to confusion of thinking processes which is reflected in his communications with others. This serial invalidation hypothesis is consistent with the 'double bind' hypothesis of Bateson *et al.* (1956), which views schizophrenia as a disturbance resulting from conflicting messages being transmitted from the parent to the child. Unfortunately for this construct model however, Bannister *et al.* (1971) have been unable to demonstrate experimentally that invalidation does in fact lead to a significant loosening of constructs.

*Assessment.* PCT has given rise to an assessment technique which combines the flexible idiographic qualities of projective techniques with the tangibility and manageability of questionnaire data. The *repertory grid technique* is currently used by many who favour behaviour therapy, psychotherapy and drug therapy, because it combines these two hitherto irreconcilable characteristics. The great interest in this assessment approach has inevitably led to modifications and sophistications, but it is only possible here to consider briefly the traditional technique as described by Kelly. The following steps are involved in obtaining a general picture of the individual's repertoire of constructs:

1. The individual is asked to write down the names of twenty or so people who are important in his life (*elements*).
2. He is then given three of the names and is asked to say in what way two are similar and differ from the third. His answer (e.g. 'these two are kind whereas he is cruel') indicates the *construct* that he is using (i.e. kind-cruel).

3. This construct is applied across all the elements.
4. This process is repeated with different groups of elements until an exhaustive list of constructs has been elicited.
5. The psychologist then creates a matrix, using this data, with the elements determining the columns and the constructs the rows.
6. In the body of the table, he writes down single digit binary numbers (i.e. '1' and '0') according to the way in which each of the elements is regarded in terms of each of the constructs.

Having collected this data, various statistical analyses can be carried out to determine, for instance, the individual's mode of construing, and the way he regards the important people in his life. Thus the matrix can be factor-analysed to see whether the person is using a wide variety of constructs (i.e. a loose system) or a small number operating in many guises (i.e. a rigid system). Another point which can be looked for is to see whether the client uses many constructs when dealing with certain classes of people (e.g. members of his family) and much fewer with others. Additional clinically-relevant information can be obtained by examining the similarities in the ways that various of the elements are construed. For instance it may be interesting to find that the client wants to marry someone who is construed as being identical to his mother, or that he sees himself as being like his father whom he despises. For some examples of the ways in which information can be gleaned from grids and utilized in treatment programmes, the reader is referred to Fransella (1971).

*Methods of effecting change.* After the refreshingly different flavour of the theory and the elegance of the assessment technique, psychotherapy along PCT lines turns out to be rather disappointing. The basic aim here is to produce changes in the internal organization of the client so that he will be able to make sense out of his world. Thus if the individual is found to be a tight construer, then the construct therapist will utilize such psychoanalytic techniques as free association and dream interpretation, or the fantasy techniques of Gestalt therapy, or reflective listening of the Rogerian variety. The loose construer, on the other hand, will have his constructs tightened up by behaviour therapy methods (e.g. hierarchy building) or by completing and analysing repertory grids.

The only truly original treatment device to emerge from

the PCT stable is *fixed role therapy*. The client is first of all asked to write a self-characterization in the third person. The therapist then makes use of this in order to create a 'fixed role sketch' which he will ask the client to role play. Ideally this fictitious character should lie somewhere between the client's self-portrait and its exact opposite. The rough draft is then shown to the client who can request that it be modified if he finds himself unable to 'believe in' or accept the character he is going to adopt. When the task is completed to the satisfaction of both parties, the client is requested to 'be' this fictitious person for a period of three weeks. The aim of this quite arduous exercise is to demonstrate to the client that he has the ability to act, think and feel differently, and that the feed-back he receives will vary according to his actions. In other words he learns that his construct system can, in fact, undergo change. According to Bannister, fixed-role therapy is a device which should only be used occasionally as a means of making a point to the client. It is not a treatment programme in itself.

*Critical appraisal.* PCT has been widely criticized on the grounds that it is too mentalistic. The ideal rational man, as depicted by Kelly and Bannister, seems more like a counter-programmed robot than a human being who is capable of intense emotional experience. True, Kelly provided some rather ingenious explanations of anxiety, hostility, guilt, fear and aggression, which have convinced Bannister at least that this mentalistic charge is unfounded. Thus hostility, for instance, is regarded as the feeling we experience when a prediction we are continually trying to confirm keeps being invalidated. When this happens, we tend to bully people in order to get them to behave in line with our constructs. Such a description of a complex emotion is generally considered, by psychoanalysts in particular, to be both too vague and too mechanistic. Indeed, even those who are by no means ill-disposed towards PCT in the main, feel that the element of emotion is outside the range of convenience of the theory.

Idiographic psychologists, such as Rogerians, while being attracted by the apparently individual orientation of the theory and techniques, have been unimpressed by Bannister's pre-occupations with 'thought-disordered schizophrenics' and other formal diagnostic categories he has experimented on. They feel that Kelly's original conceptualizations have, to a certain extent, been prostituted by the attempts of some

128

workers to make generalizations about the sorts of construct systems which are characteristic of each of the syndromes covered by the neo-Kraepelian system.

Perhaps the main weakness of PCT lies in the fact that it has failed to give rise to a clearly defined school of psycho-therapy. The treatment approach would seem to consist of a diverse assortment of plagiarized techniques which are administered to clients in a fairly *ad hoc* manner. The impression one has of the construct therapist is of a woolly-minded eclectic who is using his modifications of techniques he has not received training in, on a trial-and-error basis, with only a vague suggestion from the grid as to whether he should start with deep psychoanalysis or systematic desensitization. Certainly, in view of the painstakingly precise quality of the vast repertory grid literature, the few reports that exist on how to conduct construct therapy are so vague and trivial as to lead one to have serious doubts as to whether the assessment and treatment techniques are in fact conceptually related at all.

## Summary and conclusions

Undoubtedly the popularity of PCT is due mainly to the fact that it combines intellectual 'meat' with flexibility, humanitarianism and scientific respectability. Many psychologists who have been unable to accept the assumptions of psycho-analytic theory, and who have deplored the reductionistic and mechanistic nature of behaviour therapy, have found the structured cognitive approach of Kelly to be more in accordance with their view of what psychology should be about. A second reason for its popularity is that it is not primarily concerned with either emotions or behaviour and therefore does not directly threaten the major schools. Thus even committed psychoanalysts and behaviour therapists have been strangely loath to attack PCT, presumably because many of its tenets are by no means inconsistent with their own theories. The Freudian ego, for instance, could quite conceivably be presented as using constructs in its dealings with reality. Similarly, few behaviourists would disagree with the view that cognitive changes follow behavioural ones, and furthermore would probably regard the PCT explanation as being as acceptable as any that have been proposed. However both these schools consider cognitive processes to be of relatively minor importance and would be quick to dispute the central place assigned to them by followers of PCT.

As a school in its own right, PCT has been noted mainly for the refreshingly different viewpoint it has given the clinician, and the sophisticated forms of measurement which have emerged from it. As yet, however, it has failed to give rise to a distinct brand of psychological intervention of proven efficacy. Nevertheless it is one of the growing schools of thought and it is too soon to make any final judgements on it at this stage.

## Conclusions

Few would doubt that psychiatry and clinical psychology are going through a transitional period. The medical model, while still the dominant one in this field, is currently under attack from such diverse sources as humanism, psycho-analysis, behaviourism and existentialism. The psychosocially-inclined are critical of the rigidity of the categorization system, the assumption that the genesis of disorders is at least partially physiological, and the insensitiveness and crudity of the treatment approach which aims to suppress the signs and symptoms rather than to deal with the individual as a person in its own right. Others have pointed out that traditional psychiatry is intimately bound up with a system of values, and that clinicians who practise in this way are really agents of society who are suppressing non-conformists under the guise of medicine. Perhaps the most serious charge levied against the medical model is that it has ceased to develop. The only new research findings these days are those concerned with new psychotropic drugs which purport to eliminate symptoms more effectively, and give rise to fewer side effects, than their predecessors. Thus organic psychiatrists are still talking about 'neurotics' and 'psychotics' and prescribing pills and administering ECT as they have done for decades. As Kelly might have put it, it would appear that the medical model has extended the range of convenience of its constructs as far as it can. For all but the most hard-line of organic psychiatrists, this is by no means far enough.

What signs are there that the psychosocial models might fare any better in this difficult area? It must be conceded at once that none of the models described in the second part of this book is well enough developed to cope with the vast field covered by the medical model on its own. Each of them seems to operate best with certain specific types of disorders. Thus behaviourists are more effective with overt disturbances, psychoanalysts are best suited to working with suppressed emotions, PCT and client-centred therapists prefer to deal with people who are confused about themselves and the sorts of lives they are leading, and existentialists are most interested in 'psychotic' disorders. Despite the limited scope of each of these approaches, in their own areas of competence they would seem to have far more to offer than the suppressive techniques of organic psychiatry.

If the models were consistent with each other, the obvious solution to the problem of how to replace medical psychiatry would be to propose that psychosocial therapists should work side by side, each dealing with clients who fall into his particular area of expertise. However this is by no means the case and, in fact, such models as psychoanalysis and behaviourism are, in certain important respects, actually contradictory (see D3). Nevertheless, at a practical level, it is important to emphasize that there is relatively little overlap, in terms of areas of competence, between the various schools. Thus a temporary (but unsatisfactory) solution might be to suggest a form of pragmatic eclecticism, while research into the various models continues. Since Freudian man can exist by using the defence mechanism of compartmentalization, and since Kellian man can cope by employing discrete construct constellations, there would seem to be no reason why psychology and psychiatry could not act similarly. However this must be seen to be a temporary measure because, as in the case of the human analogy, internal inconsistency does not lead to either efficiency or growth potential. Whether the eventual solution will be reached by one of the clusters expanding and encapsulating the others, or by the superordinate constructs opening up points of contact between these clusters, remains to be seen. The essential thing is that eventually practical eclecticism must be replaced by a unitary conceptual system if the mysteries of psychological disturbances are ever to be fully understood and dealt with in the most appropriate manner.

Finally, the question of the actual context within which psychological assistance should be provided needs to be considered. Psychosocial therapists, with the possible exception of psychoanalysts, would agree that the mental hospital is the worst possible place for carrying out their work. The reasons they would give are diverse. For Laingians, the authoritarian rigidity of institutionalized life would prevent the inner self from developing. For behaviourists and Rogerians, the dependent role which hospital patients inevitably adopt would work against their belief that their clients should take on responsibility for change. All would strongly object to the existence of psychiatric hospitals as such because they help to reinforce the notion of social deviance which is still very much associated with the psychologically distressed. There is however no clear agreement as to what these non-organicists are proposing as an alternative. Humanists and existentialists, by and large, favour the existence of therapeutic communities which are essentially community-based, non-authoritarian and flexible. Behaviourists would prefer to work in retraining establishments located in the community which would cater for all learning difficulties ranging from mutism in the autistic child to underdeveloped negotiating skills in the business man. Construct therapists would probably offer a professional consultancy service similar to that provided by members of the legal profession. As yet these various schemes have not been properly put to the test and, in fact, the majority of practitioners of psychosocial therapies are still working in hospital environments which are not at all suited to their various approaches. Presumably the proposed ventures into the community will not be put into effect on a large scale until such time as the stigma of psychological distress has finally evaporated. It is hoped that this book has at least gone a little way towards hastening this process.

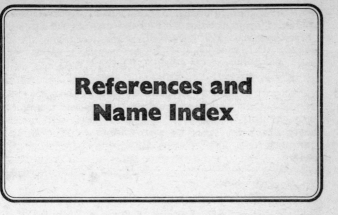

# References and Name Index

*The numbers in italics following each entry refer to page numbers within this book.*

Abse, D. W. (1959) Hysteria. In Arieti, S. (ed.) *American Handbook of Psychiatry, 1.* New York: Basic Books. *23*

Adams, M. B. (1964) Mental Illness or interpersonal behaviour. *American Psychologist 19*: 191–7. *67*

Alcock, T. (1963) *The Rorschach in Practice.* London: Tavistock. *66*

American Psychiatric Association (1968) *Diagnostic and Statistical Manual of Mental Disorders* (2nd edn). Washington D.C. *19, 20*

American Psychological Association (1970) Psychology and mental retardation. *American Psychologist 25*: 267–8. *34*

Anastasi, A. (1968) *Psychological Testing* (3rd edn). New York: Macmillan. *67, 68, 86*

Ausubel, D. P. (1961) Personality disorder *is* disease. *American Psychologist 16*: 69–74. *52*

Ayllon, T. and Azrin, N. H. (1968) *The Token Economy: A motivational system for therapy and rehabilitation.* New York: Appleton-Century-Crofts. *119*

Bandura, A. (1969) *Principles of Behaviour Modification.* New York: Holt, Rinehart and Winston. *111*

Bannister, D. (1963) The genesis of schizophrenic thought disorder: A serial invalidation hypothesis. *British Journal of Psychiatry 109*: 680–6. *77, 125, 126*

Bannister, D. (1968) The logical requirements of research into schizophrenia. *British Journal of Psychiatry 114*: 181–8. *43*

Bannister, D. (1969) Clinical psychology and psychotherapy. *Bulletin – British Psychological Society 22*: 299–301. *72, 77, 78*

Bannister, D. and Fransella, F. (1967) A grid test of schizophrenic thought disorder. *British Journal of Social and Clinical Psychology* 5: 95–102. *68, 125*

Bannister, D., Fransella, F. and Agnew, J. (1971) Characteristics and validity of the grid test of thought disorder. *British Journal of Social and Clinical Psychology* 10: 144–51. *125, 126*

Bateson, G., Jackson, D., Haley, J. and Weakland, J. (1956) Towards a theory of schizophrenia. *Behavioural Science* 4: 251–64. *126*

Baughman, E. E. (1951) Rorschach scores as a function of examiner difference. *Journal of Projective Techniques* 15: 243–9. *66*

Beck, A. T. (1962) Reliability of psychiatric diagnosis: A critique of systematic studies. *American Journal of Psychiatry* 119: 210–16. *45*

Bender, L. (1938) A visual motor Gestalt test and its clinical use. *American Orthopsychiatry Association Research Monographs 3. 69*

Breger, L. and McGaugh, J. (1965) Critique and reformulation of 'learning theory' approaches to psychotherapy and neurosis. *Psychological Bulletin* 63: 338–58. *121*

British Psychological Society (1963) Report of the working party on subnormality. *Bulletin of the British Psychological Society* 53: 37–50. *35*

Buros, O. K. (ed.) (1959) *The Fifth Mental Measurements Year Book*. New Jersey: Gryphon Press. *66*

Buss, A. H. (1966) *Psychopathology*. New York: Wiley. *45*

Cahoon, D. D. (1969) Symptom substitution and the behaviour therapies: A reappraisal. *Psychological Bulletin* 69: 149–56. *121*

Cautela, J. R. (1967) Covert sensitization. *Psychological Records* 20: 459–68. *119*

Coleman, J. C. (1972) *Abnormal Psychology and Modern Life* (4th edn). Illinois: Scott Foreman. *25*

Davis, K. (1938) Mental hygiene and the class structure. *Psychiatry* 1: 55–65. *58*

Desai, M. M. (1967) The concept of clinical psychology. *Bulletin of the British Psychological Society* 20: 29–39. *62, 63*

Elinson, J., Padilla, E. and Perkins, M. E. (1967) *Public Image of Mental Health Services*. New York: Mental Health Materials Center. *57*

Eysenck, H. J. (1960) Classification and the problem of diagnosis. In Eysenck, H. J. (ed.) *Handbook of Abnormal Psychology*. London: Pitman. *46, 109, 110*

Eysenck, H. J. (1966) *The Effects of Psychotherapy*. New York: International Science Press. *94*

Eysenck, H. J. (1972) The experimental study of Freudian concepts. *Bulletin of the British Psychological Society* 25: 261–7. *93*

Eysenck, H. J. and Rachman, S. (1965) *The Causes and Cures of Neurosis*. London: Routledge and Kegan Paul. *112*

Feldman, M. P. and McCulloch, M. J. (1965) The application of anticipatory avoidance learning to the treatment of homosexuality No. 1: Theory techniques and preliminary results. *Behavior Research and Therapy 2*: 165–83. *118*

Fiedler, F. E. (1950) A comparison of therapeutic relations in psychoanalytic, non-directive and Adlerian therapy. *Journal of Consulting Psychology 14*: 436–55. *94*

Foulds, G. A. (1955) The reliability of psychiatric and the validity of psychological diagnosis. *Journal of Mental Science 101*: 851–2 *38*

Foulds, G. A. (1961) Personality traits and neurotic symptoms and signs. *British Journal of Medical Psychology 34*: 263–70. *66*

Foulds, G. A., Hope, K., McPherson, F. M. and Mayo, P. R. (1967) Cognitive disorder among the schizophrenias 1: The validity of some tests of thought process disorder. *British Journal of Psychiatry 113*: 1361–8. *69*

Frankel, A. J. (1975) Beyond the simple functional analysis – the chain: a conceptual framework for assessment with a case study example. *Behavior Therapy 6*: 254–60. *120*

Fransella, F. (1971) *Personal Construct Psychotherapy and Stuttering*. London: Academic Press. *127*

Freud, S. (1909) *Five Lectures on Psychoanalysis*. Standard Edition 11. London: Hogarth. *87*

Freud, S. (1914) *Recollecting, Repeating and Working Through*. Standard Edition 12. London: Hogarth. *89*

Freud, S. (1920) *Beyond the Pleasure Principle*. Standard Edition 18. London: Hogarth. *88*

Freud, S. (1926) *Inhibitions, Symptoms and Anxiety*. Standard Edition 20. London: Hogarth. *88*

Geer, J. H. (1965) The development of a scale to measure fear. *Behavior Research and Therapy 3*: 45–53. *115*

Gibb, J. R. (1970) The effects of human relations training. In A. E. Bergin and S. L. Garfield (eds) *Handbook of Psychotherapy and Behaviour Change*. New York: Wiley. *101, 102*

Gobetz, W. (1953) A quantitive standardization and validation of the Bender–Gestalt test on normal and neurotic adults. *Psychological Monographs 67, No. 6. 69*

Goldstein, M. J., Judd, K. K., Rodnick, E. H. and La Polla, A., (1969) Psychophysiological and behavioural effects of phenothiazine administration in acute schizophrenics as a function of pre-morbid states. *Journal of Psychiatric Research 6*: 271–87.

Gordon, J. S. (1971) Who is mad? Who is sane? R. D. Laing: In search of a new psychiatry. *Atlantic 227*: 50–6. *106*

Greenson, R. R. (1965) The working alliance and the transference neurosis. *Psychoanalytic Quarterly 34*: 155–81. *87*

Hathaway, S. R. and McKinley, J. C. (1951) *Minnesota Multi-*

*phasic Personality Inventory. Revised Edition.* New York: Psychological Corporation. *67*

Hathaway, S. R. and Meehl, P. E. (1951) *An Atlas for the Clinical Use of the M.M.P.I.* Minneapolis: University of Minnesota Press. *67*

Jahoda, M. (1958) *Current Concepts of Positive Mental Health.* New York: Basic Books. *52, 53*

Kanfer, F. H. and Phillips, J. (1970) *Learning Foundations and Behavior Therapy.* New York: Wiley. *45*

Kendall, R. E. (1968) *The Classification of Depressive Illness.* London: Oxford University Press. *22*

Kleinmuntz, B. (1974) *Essentials of Abnormal Psychology.* New York: Harper and Row. *65*

Kline, P. (1972) *Fact and Fantasy in Freudian Theory.* London: Methuen. *93*

Kraepelin, E. (1913) *Psychiatry* (8th edn) Leipzig: Thieme. *18, 28, 29, 44, 48, 49, 50, 72*

Laing, R. D. (1960) *The Divided Self.* London: Tavistock. *96, 103–6*

Lief, A. (ed.) (1948) *The Commonsense Psychiatry of Dr Adolf Meyer.* New York: McGraw-Hill. *48*

Lipinski, D. and Nelson, R. (1974) Problems in the use of naturalistic observation as a means of behavioural assessment. *Behavior Therapy 5*: 341–51. *116*

McGuire, R. J., Carlisle, J. M. and Young, B. G. (1965) Sexual deviations as conditioned behaviour: a hypothesis. *Behaviour Research and Therapy 2*: 185–90. *114*

McNemar, Q. (1957) On WAIS difference scores. *Journal of Consulting Psychology 21*: 239–40. *68*

Maher, B. A. (1970) *Introduction to Research in Psychopathology.* New York: McGraw-Hill. *46*

Makhlouf-Norris, F., Jones, H. G. and Norris, H. (1970) Articulation of the conceptual structure in obsessional neurosis. *British Journal of Social and Clinical Psychology 9*: 264–74. *125*

Malinowski, B. (1927) *Sex and Repression in Savage Society.* London: Kegan Paul. *92*

Malmo, R. B. (1970) Emotions and muscle tension: the story of Anne. *Psychology Today 3*: 64. *23*

Maslow, A. H. (1970) *Motivation and Personality* (2nd edn). New York: Harper and Row. *52, 53*

Masters, W. H. and Johnson, V. E. (1970) *Human Sexual Inadequacy.* Boston: Little and Brown. *55*

Mednick, S. A. (1970) Breakdown in individuals at high risk for schizophrenia: possibly pre-dispositional perinatal factors. *Journal of Mental Hygiene 54*: 50–63. *77*

Meehl, P. E. (1959) Some ruminations on the validation of clinical procedures. *Canadian Journal of Psychology 13*: 103–28. *46*

Meichenbaum, D. H. (1973) Cognitive factors in behaviour

modification: modifying what clients say to themselves. In R. D. Rubin, J. P. Brady and J. D. Henderson (eds) *Advances in Behaviour Therapy*, 4. New York: Academic Press. *122*

Mischel, W. (1968) *Personality and Assessment*. New York: Wiley. *115*

Parry-Jones W., Santer-Westrate, H. G. and Crawley, R. C. (1970) Behaviour therapy in a case of hysterical blindness. *Behavior Research and Therapy 8*: 79–85. *23*

Pascal, G. R. and Suttell, B. J. (1951) *The Bender–Gestalt Test: Quantification and Validity for Adults*. New York: Grune and Stratton. *69*

Patterson, C. H. (1953) *The Wechsler–Bellevue Scales: a guide for counselors*. Illinois: Thomas. *68*

Paul, G. L. (1966) *Insight Versus Desensitization in Psychotherapy: An Experiment in Anxiety Reduction*. Stanford: Stanford University Press. *77, 95*

Poole, A. D. (1968) *Retrospective Investigation of the Clinical Usefulness of the Bannister–Fransella Grid Test of Schizophrenic Thought Disorder*. Unpub. M.Sc. Thesis: University of London. *69*

Rabin, A. I. and Guertin, W. H. (1951) Research with the Wechsler–Bellevue test: 1945–1950. *Psychological Bulletin 48*: 211–48. *68*

Rachman, S. (1966) Sexual fetishism: an experimental analogue. *Psychological Records 16*: 293–6. *112, 114*

Rachman, S. and Teasdale, J. (1969) *Aversion Therapy and Behaviour Disorders: An Analysis*. Coral Gables: University of Miami Press. *119*

Rogers, C. R. (1959) A theory of therapy, personality and inter-personal relationships, as developed in the client centered framework in S. Koch's (ed.) *Psychology: A Study of a Science*. Study I: *Conceptual and Systematic*, Vol. 3 *Formulations of the Persons and the Social Context*. New York: McGraw-Hill. *96–99*

Rogers, C. R. (1965) *Client Centered Therapy*. New York: Houghton Mifflin. *100*

Rogers, C. R. (1970) *Carl Rogers on Encounter Groups*. New York: Harper and Row. *101*

Rogers, C. R. and Dymond, R. F. (eds) (1954) *Psychotherapy and Personality Change*. Chicago: University of Chicago Press. *38, 100*

Rosenhahn, D. L. (1973) On being sane in insane places. *Science 179*: 250–8. *39*

Sandler, J., Dare, C. and Holder, A. (1970) Basic psychoanalytic concepts: III. Transference. *British Journal of Psychiatry 116*: 667–72. *87, 89*

Sarbin, T. R. (1967) On the futility of the proposition that some people be labelled 'mentally ill'. *Journal of Consulting Psychology 31*: 447–53. *58*

Sarbin, T. R. and Mancuso, J. C. (1970) Failure of a moral

enterprise. *Journal of Clinical and Consulting Psychology 35*: 159–73. *57*

Schafer, R. (1948) *The Clinical Application of Psychological Tests.* New York: International University Press. *68*

Schmidt, H. O. and Fonda, C. (1956) The reliability of psychiatric diagnosis. *Journal of Abnormal and Social Psychology 52*: 262–7. *45*

Scodel, A. (1957) Heterosexual somatic preference and fantasy dependence. *Journal of Consulting Psychology 21*: 371–4. *92*

Seligman, M. E. P. (1973) *Helplessness. On Depression, Development and Death.* San Francisco: Freeman. *114, 115*

Seligman, M. E. P. and Maier, S. F. (1967) Failure to escape traumatic shock. *Journal of Experimental Psychology 74*: 1–9. *76*

Slater, E. and Roth, M. (1969) *Clinical Psychiatry* (3rd edn). London: Baillière, Tindall and Cassell. *16, 22, 25, 29, 36, 48, 78*

Smail, D. J. (1973) Clinical psychology and the medical model. *Bulletin of the British Psychological Society 26*: 211–14. *72, 79*

Snaith, R. P. (1968) A clinical investigation of phobias. *British Journal of Psychiatry 114*: 673–97. *21*

Stampfl, T. G. and Levis, D. J. (1967) Essentials of implosive therapy: a learning-theory-based psycho-dynamic behaviour therapy. *Journal of Abnormal and Social Psychology 72*: 496–503. *117*

Szasz, T. S. (1957) On the theory of psychoanalytic treatment. *International Journal of Psychoanalysis 38*: 166–82. *48*

Szasz, T. S. (1960) The myth of mental illness. *American Psychologist 15*: 113–18. *9, 52, 56, 57*

Szasz, T. S. (1966) The psychiatric classification of behaviour: a strategy of personal constraint. In L. D. Eron (ed.) *The Classification of Behaviour Disorders.* Chicago: Aldine. *42*

Toler, A. and Schulberg, H. (1963) *An Evaluation of the Bender–Gestalt Test.* Illinois: Thomas. *71*

Truax, C. B. (1966) Reinforcement and non-reinforcement in Rogerian psychotherapy. *Journal of Abnormal and Social Psychology 71*: 1–9. *102*

Truax, C. B. and Carkhuff, R. R. (1964) Significant developments in psychotherapy research. In L. E. Abt and B. F. Reiss (eds) *Progress in Clinical Psychology.* New York: Grune and Stratton. *100*

Vaillant, G. (1966) The prediction of recovery in schizophrenia. *International Journal of Psychiatry 1*: 617–24. *77*

Venables, P. H. (1963) The relationship between the level of skin potential and fusion of paired light flashes in schizophrenic and normal subjects. *Journal of Psychiatric Research 1*: 279–82. *31*

Walton, D. W. and Black, D. A. (1957) The validity of a psychological test of brain damage. *British Journal of Medical Psychology 30*: 270–2. *70*

Watson, J. B. and Rayner, R. (1920) Conditioned emotional reactions. *Journal of Experimental Psychology 3*: 1–14. *112*

Wechsler, D. (1955) *Manual for the Wechsler Adult Intelligence Scale*. New York: Psychological Corporation. *67*

Wechsler, D. (1958) *The Measurement and Appraisal of Adult Intelligence* (4th edn). Baltimore: Williams and Wilkins. *68*

Wilson, M. S. and Meyer, E. (1962) Diagnostic consistency in the psychiatric liaison service. *American Journal of Psychiatry 119*: 207–9. *46*

Wittenborn, J. (1951) Symptom patterns in a group of mental hospital patients. *Journal of Consulting Psychology 15*: 290–302. *43*

Wolpe, J. (1958) *Psychotherapy by Reciprocal Inhibition*. Stanford: Stanford University Press. *116, 117*

Wolpe, J. (1968) Learning therapies. In J. G. Howels (ed.) *Modern Perspectives in World Psychiatry*. Edinburgh: Oliver and Boyd. *109*

Yalom, I. D. and Liebermann, M. A. (1971) A Study of encounter group casualties. *Archives of General Psychiatry 25*: 16–30. *102*

Zigler, E. and Phillips, L. (1961) Psychiatric diagnosis: A critique. *Journal of Abnormal and Social Psychology 63*: 607–8. *43*

Zilboorg, G. and Henry, G. W. (1941) *A History of Medical Psychology*. New York: Norton. *50*

# Subject Index